Health Behavior Change in Response to HIV/AIDS in Ghana

Augustine Amenyah

Health Behavior Change in Response to HIV/AIDS in Ghana

HIV/AIDS and Health Education in Contemporary
Societies: The Case of Ghana

LAP LAMBERT Academic Publishing

Impressum / Imprint

Bibliografische Information der Deutschen Nationalbibliothek: Die Deutsche Nationalbibliothek verzeichnet diese Publikation in der Deutschen Nationalbibliografie; detaillierte bibliografische Daten sind im Internet über http://dnb.d-nb.de abrufbar. Alle in diesem Buch genannten Marken und Produktnamen unterliegen warenzeichen-, marken- oder patentrechtlichem Schutz bzw. sind Warenzeichen oder eingetragene Warenzeichen der jeweiligen Inhaber. Die Wiedergabe von Marken, Produktnamen, Gebrauchsnamen, Handelsnamen, Warenbezeichnungen u.s.w. in diesem Werk berechtigt auch ohne besondere Kennzeichnung nicht zu der Annahme, dass solche Namen im Sinne der Warenzeichen- und Markenschutzgesetzgebung als frei zu betrachten wären und daher von jedermann benutzt werden dürften.

Bibliographic information published by the Deutsche Nationalbibliothek: The Deutsche Nationalbibliothek lists this publication in the Deutsche Nationalbibliografie; detailed bibliographic data are available in the Internet at http://dnb.d-nb.de. Any brand names and product names mentioned in this book are subject to trademark, brand or patent protection and are trademarks or registered trademarks of their respective holders. The use of brand names, product names, common names, trade names, product descriptions etc. even without a particular marking in this works is in no way to be construed to mean that such names may be regarded as unrestricted in respect of trademark and brand protection legislation and could thus be used by anyone.

Coverbild / Cover image: www.ingimage.com

Verlag / Publisher:
LAP LAMBERT Academic Publishing
ist ein Imprint der / is a trademark of
AV Akademikerverlag GmbH & Co. KG
Heinrich-Böcking-Str. 6-8, 66121 Saarbrücken, Deutschland / Germany
Email: info@lap-publishing.com

Herstellung: siehe letzte Seite /
Printed at: see last page
ISBN: 978-3-659-22300-6

Zugl. / Approved by: Athens, GA University of Georgia, Diss., 2005

TABLE OF CONTENTS

Page

CHAPTER

LIST OF FIGURES

CHAPTER ONE

INTRODUCTION

Background of the Problem

The Joint United Nations Program on HIV/AIDS (UNAIDS, 2005a) reported that as of

December 2003, an estimated 40 million people were living with HIV/AIDS in the world.

Nearly 60 million people have contracted the virus since 1981 when HIV/AIDS appeared in

public health according to the Centers for Disease Control and Prevention, (CDC, 1981). The

virus is the fourth largest killer in the world and the leading cause of death in Africa (UNAIDS,

2005a). About thirty-four and one half million adults and 1.2 million children were living with

HIV by the end of 2003. Currently, about 24.5 million people with HIV/AIDS reside in Africa

(UNAIDS, 2005b).

The epidemic is spreading in a number of countries in Africa. In Botswana, 1 in 3 young

women and 1 in 7 young men aged 15 to 24 are infected with HIV, as are 1 in 4 young women

and 1 in 10 young men in Lesotho, South Africa, and Zimbabwe. It is further estimated that in

Ivory Coast, 10 percent of the sexually active population is infected and about 2.2 million people

are HIV positive in Nigeria (Umeh, 1999). Uganda, Botswana, Kenya, Tanzania, Zambia, and

South Africa are infamous for HIV/AIDS in Africa. The situation is no different for Ghana,

Liberia, Burkina-Faso, and Togo where more than 10 percent of pregnant women are infected

(UNICEF Progress of Nations, 2000).

1

Differential rates have been reported for urban and rural areas and among women and men (Mann, Tarantola & Netter, 1996). For example, Uganda's capital city of Kampala has a 20 percent rate of infection for pregnant women in comparison to five percent for those in Rakai District. Similarly, in Zambia the sero prevalence rate for women attending Sexually Transmitted Disease (STD) Centers was higher than men attending similar clinics. These differentials rates between men and women may be due to the fact that men in Africa do not avail themselves to HIV/AIDS testing, whereas women who are pregnant are tested for HIV/AIDS. In addition the rural urban disparities in prevalence figures may also be explained by differentials rates of accessibility to health and medical services. People in the rural areas do not have access to proper medical testing for HIV/AIDS, whereas people in the urban centers do.

Nowhere has HIV/AIDS been so devastating than in Africa, where whole families and villages have succumbed to the epidemic. Many writers have compared HIV/AIDS to the Bubonic plague of medieval Europe that killed over 50 percent of the population (Feldman, 1990; Mann, Tarantola & Netter, 1996; Umeh, 1999). European society, belief systems, and the general understanding of public health are reported to have changed due to the medieval plague. Unfortunately women, lepers, and non-Christians who were thought to have spread the plague were attacked (Gottfried, 1983). In addition, the effects were tragically felt all across Europe. Likewise today, the effects of HIV/AIDS is being felt all over Africa in homes, schools, hospitals, markets, farms, and in government offices.

The overall rate of infection for adults in Africa is 8.8 percent, compared to 1.1 percent in other regions according to UNAIDS (2005b). The rate of infection for women is also reported to be higher than men. For example, women make up 53 percent of the infected adult population in the region compared to only four percent in North America (UNAIDS, 2005a).

Major impacts of the disease have been noted in the areas of economic, social

development, and politics. Economic loss affects mostly the productive sector where people

living with HIV/AIDS (PLWA) may perform below expected capacity. Agricultural production

at both the individual and national levels has been reduced due to HIV/AIDS (AIDS in Africa,

Washington Post, December 12, 1999). The most affected groups are adults who are between the

ages of 15 to 49 years old - the group considered the most productive economically.

AIDS deaths have affected particularly skilled workers whose replacements are hard to

find. Shortages of veteran teachers and workers in many countries have been blamed on the

illness. In Ivory Coast five teachers die every week of the school year and in Zambia 1,300

teachers died due to AIDS in 1999 (Congressional Research Services Report, 2002). The

pandemic has been devastating to health care workers who, due to lack of proper training and

lack of equipment, have misdiagnosed HIV as malaria and they too have contracted the disease

(Orubuloye, 1993; Umeh, 1999).

Due to poverty the already inadequate health care delivery system has been over-

burdened by new cases of HIV/AIDS. In addition, many communities have been totally wiped

out due to AIDS and it is feared that if nothing is done to stem the tide, population growth would

be affected (Mann, Tarantola & Netter, 1996).

Deaths from AIDS have resulted especially in poor agricultural production leading to the

loss of income at the micro and macro economic and social levels. Since all of Africa depends

on agricultural production, there is an urgent need for governments to address this human

catastrophe. Prevention and control will lead to decline in deaths and improvement in the welfare

of people. There are also social consequences from the onset of HIV/AIDS. For example, in

Africa the majority of the populations are illiterates and, superstitious about diseases, so the

3

stigma of HIV infection is unbearable for many families who have lost loved ones to AIDS. The

Panos Institute (1999) reported that in South Africa, people suspected of having HIV/AIDS were

banished from their communities.

HIV reported cases in Western developed nations comes from varied sources such as

injection from drug use, needle exchange, unprotected sexual intercourse, and blood

transfusions. Most cases in Africa are principally transmitted through heterosexual intercourse

(Anarfi, 1993; Mann, Tarantola & Netter, 1996; Orubuloye, 1993). Furthermore, Orubuloye

(1993) reported that 90 percent of HIV cases in Africa are transmitted through heterosexual sex,

while mother to child transmission, and infection from blood transfusion accounted for only 10

percent of new infections.

Even though governments in Africa have recognized that behavioral change about sexual

habits is important to slowing the disease, most health departments lack the money, personnel,

and equipment to diagnose and offer counseling to affected people (Feldman, 1990; Mann,

Tarantola & Netter, 1996). To help fight HIV/AIDS, African governments have depended on

western developed nations with experience in fighting HIV/AIDS and who reported success at

slowing the rate of infection among vulnerable groups. For example, Atkin and Rice (2001)

reported behavioral change due to mass media health promotion campaigns. However,

indigenous customs and traditions, perceptions, attitudes, and beliefs about diseases and

HIV/AIDS coupled with scarce resources to buy antiretroviral drugs posed major challenges to

governments about how to tackle HIV/AIDS in Africa (Hope, 1999).

Mass health education campaigns have been undertaken to make people aware of the

disease (Feldman, 1990). This led to the adoption of public health education program models

from Western developed nations such as the United States and Canada (Neequaye, 1988;

4

Neequaye, Neequaye, & Biggar; 1991). For example, condoms as a safer sex strategy were promoted, so were health changing strategies based on public service announcements, radio, television, and printed media.

In order to fight the new disease through education, African countries in conjunction with the United Nations Organization have established national AIDS control programs. These national AIDS control programs formulated policies on HIV/AIDS, designed instructional curricula, developed radio and television programs, and managed other public service educational programs aimed at slowing the epidemic (Mann, Tarantola & Netter, 1996). These national AIDS control programs are not the only actors in the HIV/AIDS fight. Other actors include church organizations, community action groups, and non-governmental organizations (NGOs). The next section examines the onset of HIV/AIDS in one African country.

The conditions of HIV/AIDS patients in Ghana are varied but similar. Many people living with AIDS do not openly acknowledge the disease. Societal stigma is so strong that deaths due to AIDS have been ruled "other causes" to avoid disgrace to family members (Neequaye, 1988; Neequaye et al., 1991). Access to health care is either absent or minimal for people living with HIV/AIDS. The Ministry of Health of Ghana lamented in 2004, that the cost of providing health care for HIV/AIDS patients overburdens its health expenditure (Ghana News Agency, 2004).

Initially Ghanaian women with foreign travel experience were the hardest hit by HIV/AIDS. According to Anarfi (1993), this led many people to believe that HIV was foreign to Ghana and principally a woman's ailment. Also, Herbalists and other traditional healers claimed to have found a "cure" for AIDS. This led many people to believe that if contracted they could be cured by herbalists. Traditional practices like polygamy, puberty rites, and festivals that

5

promote sexual promiscuity also lead to further spread (Awusabo-Asare, 1995). The conditions

of people living with AIDS are appalling as health care is terribly lacking. Due to poverty, life-

prolonging medicines such as antiretroviral drugs are virtually absent.

According to Anarfi (1993), the first case of AIDS in Ghana occurred in 1986. At the

onset of the disease most of the cases were attributed to commercial sex workers who had lived

in neighboring countries especially Ivory Coast, Burkina-Faso, Togo, and Nigeria (Konotey-

Ahulu, 1989). In January 1992, 6,009 HIV cases appeared in the country, of which 4,075 were

females (68 percent). According to Anarfi and Antwi (1993), by July 1993, the number of HIV

positive cases doubled to 11,940 and that of AIDS cases tripled to 10,285. In 1999, UNICEF's

Progress of Nations reported an estimated 330,000 adults with HIV in Ghana, an increase of

more than 80 percent since 1986.

In 2004, the Ghana News Agency reported that the Ministry of Health of Ghana (MOH)

had recorded over half a million people living with HIV and AIDS in Ghana. Due to several

reasons including under reporting, under diagnosis, delayed reporting, HIV cases not coming to

health centers or hospitals, the actual statistics of HIV/AIDS cases are hard to determine and may

be much higher. To combat the staggering cases of HIV/AIDS and in line with recommendations

by the United Nations Organization (UN), the Ghana National AIDS Control program was

established in 1987.

The Ghana National AIDS Control Program (NACP) is the principal government

agency responsible for HIV/AIDS education in Ghana. Educational delivery methods used by the

NACP include posters depicting the horrors of HIV/AIDS, the modes of transmissions, and

factors that predispose people to HIV/AIDS. Other methods are radio and television broadcast,

pamphlets on methods of acquisition, and testing and counseling of AIDS patients (Awusabo-

6

Asare, 1997). Billboard advertisements that encourage the use of condoms and the social marketing of condoms as a safer sex method are popular in Ghana.

Unfortunately, HIV/AIDS reported cases continue to grow in Ghana (Anarfi, 2000; Awusabo-Asare, 1997; Bosompra, 1998; UNAIDS, 2005a). Currently, Ghana has a seroprevalence rate of 5.5 percent, which according to UNAIDS (2005a) is the threshold of severity. It appears that the educational programs formulated to combat HIV are either inadequate or are not working well to achieve the goals for which they were designed. One study that underpins this speculation is McCombie and Anarfi's (1992) study of AIDS awareness campaign in Ghana. They found that an increased level of awareness among Ghanaian adults did not translate into adaptation of safer sex behaviors.

One possible reason may be that there is something about the educational programs that the population does not comprehend to enable them to make changes to their behavior. For example, it may be that there is a disjuncture between what the people are hearing about these programs from government, and other actors in the HIV/AIDS fight as opposed to the intent of the educational programs.

Perhaps the current education format used is incongruent with Ghanaian cultural practices. One research finding that underscores this point is Panford, Nyaney, Amoah Opoku, and Garbrah Aidoo (2001) study of folk media in Ghana as the possible medium for HIV/AIDS education and behavior change intervention among a group of Ghanaian adults. They found that folk media was an important communication tool that was based on local language and traditions which were persuasive and could be adapted to carry-out health education in Ghana.

Nevertheless, the qualified success of preventive education in Africa reported by Ugugi, Simonseon, and Bosine (1999) underscores the importance of behavior change as an effective

7

strategy for the control and preventive of HIV/AIDS. Unfortunately, the United States assistance

in fighting HIV/AIDS in Africa excludes some forms of education such as condom use and

upholds abstinence only programs that have proven unsuccessful in Africa. The rationale for this

approach is that Africa has been positioned as a continent where people are promiscuous. This is

what Hill (2004) refers to as moralizing the HIV/AIDS debate. Furthermore, behavioral change

based education in some countries in Africa demonstrates that not all is lost in slowing down the

epidemic through education (Rwegera, 1999). Ugugi, Simonseon, and Bosine (1999) reported

that behavioral change programs have successfully been applied to slow the epidemic in Uganda

and Kenya.

Statement of the Problem

Learning in adulthood has been intriguing to educators since the turn of the century

(Friere, 1972; Houle, 1964; Knowles, 1980; Lindeman, 1926; Thorndike, Bregman, Tilton &

Woodyard, 1928; Tough, 1971). Recent studies by Dench and Regan (1999) have demonstrated

the benefits of learning for improved health and general well being. The quest to understand how

adults learn to make changes in their lives in response to health crises is therefore important and

a necessary step in the fight against HIV/AIDS and consequently improved health. However,

since the advent of HIV/AIDS, few studies have examined learning associated with HIV/AIDS

(Courtenay, Merriam & Reeves, 1999; Baumgartner, Courtenay, Merriam, & Reeves, 2000).

There is a gap in our understanding of how adults learn to make changes in their sexual

behaviors in response to the HIV/AIDS crisis.

A search of the literature on AIDS in Ghana using Dissertation Abstracts, ProQuest Data

base, and the search descriptors, AIDS in Ghana, AIDS in Africa, AIDS in developing world,

Ghana/HIV statistics, produced many studies documenting the prevalence of HIV/AIDS (Anarfi,

Hornik, & McCombie, 2001; Anarfi & McCombie, 1992; Awusabo-Asare, 1997; Bosompra, 1998; Panford et al., 2001). There is however, a paucity of research on how Ghanaian adults learn to change their sexual practices in response to the HIV/AIDS crisis.

This researcher was not able to locate any studies that might illuminate our understanding of the factors important for making changes in the lives of adults for successful AIDS education. Given the paucity of research in this area, this study will fill that knowledge gap by examining how Ghanaian adults learn about HIV/AIDS, and how they learn to make changes in their sexual practices in response to the AIDS epidemic.

The Purpose of the Study

The purpose of this study was to understand how Ghanaian adults learned to make changes in their sexual practices in response to the HIV/AIDS crisis. This investigation addressed the following questions:

1)   What changes have Ghanaian adults made in their sexual practices since learning about HIV/AIDS?

2)   How do Ghanaian adults learn formally or informally what they need to know to make changes in their sexual practices in response to the HIV/AIDS menace?

3)   What is the learning process that leads Ghanaian adults to change their sexual practices in response to the HIV/AIDS epidemic?

4)   What other factors encourage or deter Ghanaian adults from making changes in their sexual practices in response to the HIV/AIDS crises?

Significance of the Study

This study is significant in the area of adult learning. Though life can be prolonged through HIV/AIDS drugs, not many Ghanaians can afford these drugs because of their socio-

9

economic status. AIDS patients in Ghana are poor, and are dependent on the government for their health care needs because of lack of insurance. At the global level, poverty may be explained in terms of the effects of globalization and dependency theory. In addition, at the 2002 World AIDS Conference in Spain, scientists revealed that the African strain of HIV was resistant to all current protease inhibitors and cocktail drugs (World AIDS Conference, 2002). It is important to understand why in spite of all these mass educational programs many people still do not change sexual practices that pre-dispose them to HIV/AIDS. An understanding of the factors and processes associated with learning about HIV/AIDS and behavior change enables adult educators to appropriately design and tailor mass educational programs on HIV/AIDS. This study adds to our understanding of how people learn to make changes in their lives and the processes involved in change and decision-making. In addition, this study increases our understanding of factors that influenced the adoption of knowledge to change behavior.

Furthermore, knowledge gained from this study impacts the theoretical understanding of learning in adulthood especially from an African perspective. From research in the west, we know that radio, television, public service announcements, billboards, and printed media have been used to influence health behavior (Atkin & Rice, 2001; Elder, 2001; McGuire, 1981). However, in African societies that have large populations of traditional adults, the issue of relevance of these mass public educational tools becomes problematic for AIDS educators.

The literature on HIV/AIDS education is replete with stories about illiteracy, superstition, and the stigma of AIDS, as some of the challenges that educators face in Africa. At the beginning of the epidemic, stigma of the disease was a major deterrent to people in trying to learn about the disease. Now due to education and the on-going shift in the culture, stigma of the disease is now a major impetus for people to rather learn about the disease because of the need to

10

avoid the stigma. Therefore the barriers to health and behavior change need to be examined if

educational programs are to be effective in making changes in the lives of adults. Mass media

health promotion campaigns may need to investigate the interest of recipients if change in

perceptions, attitudes, and beliefs and behavior about AIDS are to occur. Since culture informs

language, health beliefs, and perceptions about life and hence diseases, it is important that factors

specific to HIV/AIDS, especially how people learned about the disease and how they learned to

make personal changes about sexual practices be examined in specific cultural milieu that is

grappling with high incidences of HIV/AIDS such as Ghana.

Definitions

The following are key definitions for this study.

1. PLWA: People living with AIDS.

2. UNAIDS: Joint United Nations Program on AIDS, an umbrella organization of the

   United Nations Organization fighting HIV/AIDS.

3. HIV: Human immunodeficiency virus. HIV mostly infects T Cells also called CD 4

   Cells. These cells are white blood cells that turn on the immune system to fight diseases.

   The presence of HIV gradually renders the human immune system incapable of

   performing its function of fighting diseases.

4. AIDS: Acquired Immune Deficiency Syndrome. This virus attacks the immune system's

   ability to fight infections. When the body's protection is lost many deadly infections

   (opportunistic diseases) develop and eventually results in death.

CHAPTER TWO

REVIEW OF RELATED LITERATURE

Introduction

The purpose of this study was to understand how Ghanaian adults learned to change their

sexual practices in response to the HIV/AIDS crisis. This investigation addressed the following

questions:

1. What changes have Ghanaian adults made in their sexual practices since learning

   about HIV/AIDS?

2. How do Ghanaian adults learn formally or informally what they need to know to

   make changes in their sexual practices in response to the HIV/AIDS crisis?

3. What is the learning process that leads Ghanaian adults to change their sexual

   practices in response to the HIV/AIDS crisis?

4. What other factors encourage or deter Ghanaian adults from making changes in their

   sexual practices in response to the HIV/AIDS crises?

This chapter presents a review of related literature based on the following outline: a brief

historical overview of the problem of HIV/AIDS, the impact of AIDS in Africa, and Ghana,

health behavior change models and research findings in the West, empirical studies of AIDS in

Ghana, mass media and behavior change. The researcher used Dissertation Abstracts

International, ProQuest Database, Google, MSN, with the descriptors AIDS in Ghana, AIDS in

Africa, AIDS in developing world and Ghana/HIV statistics.

A Brief History of the Problem

The exact origin of HIV/AIDS is still a medical mystery. Attempts in the past to trace the origin of the disease to Africa have stirred strong emotional responses from politicians and social activists in the region (Baffour-Ankomah, 1999).

The blight has been perceived negatively by many African cultures (Hope, 1999). In the early 1980s various theories were proposed to explain its origin. Some scholars believe it originated from the African monkey, whereas, some people also believed it was a germ warfare that went wrong. Due to its fatalities the disease has invoked fear among people, especially policy makers, politicians, educators, and behavior theorists. In addition, stigma and discrimination against people who have contracted the disease still remains a problem for educators.

Dr. Zhu of Aaron Diamond AIDS Research Center in New York reported in 1998, that a plasma sample of a Bantu man who died in 1959 in the Congo is reportedly the oldest confirmed case of HIV in the world. Based on this finding, scientists now believe that the virus initially spread from monkeys to humans between 1926 and 1946, when Polio vaccines were produced using monkey culture. However, the virus did not establish itself as an epidemic until 1930 in Africa (Zhu, Tuofo, Korber, Bette, Nahinias, & Andre,). If this discovery is true, then the origin of AIDS has been firmly placed in Africa, much to the chagrin of politicians and social commentators.

Physicians in the U.S.A. observed the current epidemic in the early 1980s. In 1981, the Centers for Disease Control and Prevention (CDC) reported high cases of rare forms of cancer (Kaposi Sarcoma) in otherwise healthy gay men in San Francisco and Los Angeles. Since at the time the disease only appeared in homosexuals, it was erroneously called "gay men's cancer"

13

and later gay-related immune deficiency disease (GRID).

In New York, many Haitian immigrants showed similar signs and symptoms of the new disease. Ironically, the initial reaction of the public to the new disease was that of fear and despondency shaped by discourses in the press that projected the disease as punishment for deviant lifestyles. Due to lack of information about its mode of transmission and gestation period, the media labeled groups such as immigrants, homosexuals, and injecting drug users as the source of the disease until the mid 1980s.

At the first world AIDS Conference held in Atlanta in 1985, scientists identified the principal mode of transmission as sexual intercourse, sharing of drug paraphernalia, and tainted blood transfusion. Following the first AIDS Conference, the then U.S Surgeon General Everett Koop published a report on AIDS, which called for sex education to educate the public about prevention and control of the new virus in America. Over 107 million copies of this AIDS pamphlet were mailed to households across the nation. The pamphlet contained information about modes of transmissions, and information that sought to allay the fears of people about contracting the virus through common interpersonal behavior such as kissing and insect bites.

Unprotected sexual intercourse, vertical transmission, and tainted blood transfusions are principal modes of transmission. Other risk factors for the transmission of the virus include sharing of drug paraphernalia, socio-economic factors such as migration, poverty, and polygamy (Kelly, 1994, Kelly, 1995a, Kelly, 1995b; Mann, Tarantola, & Netter, 1996; Wingwood & DiClemente1992). In Western developed nations such as the U.S., AIDS was initially localized among groups of individuals who shared a common exposure risk. For example, sexually active gay men were the first to be identified, and later drug users, and recipients of blood from blood banks (CDC, 1999).

14

On the contrary, in non-western societies, commercial sex workers, migrant workers,

cultural practices such as polygamy, and poverty are associated with the rapid spread of the virus

(Mann, Tarantola, & Netter, 1996).

Medical responses in the form of drug therapy began in early 1980s. Between 1988 and

1990, the Food and Drug Administration (FDA) approved Intron A and Referon A for the

treatment of Kaposi sarcoma and pentamidine mist for use against PCP and AZT against AIDS.

Other drug combinations are in experimental stages with promising results for making life better

for people living with the disease. Advances in medical science have been relatively beneficial

(better care, and longer meaningful life) for people living with AIDS in the West. To the

contrary, governments in Africa cannot afford the cost of these drugs (protease inhibitors,

cocktail drugs, antiretroviral) for distribution to people living with the disease due to poverty.

In 2001, major drug companies in the west declined African nations' demand for

reduced cost for anti-retroviral and protease inhibitors so as to make them affordable for their

populations. The hopes of African countries benefiting from current advances in treatment were

dashed at the 2002 AIDS Conference in Spain. At the Conference, research scientists reported

that the African strain of HIV was resistant to available antiretroviral and protease inhibitors

(World AIDS Conference, 2002). This discovery, though controversial, dealt a further blow to

efforts by many governments to provide life-prolonging care for their people in Africa through

medical approaches to prevention.

Safer sex educational approaches remain the major goal of governments for the control

and prevention of HIV/AIDS in Africa. Due to its invisible nature and a long gestational period,

the impact of AIDS may be obscure to the casual observer for a long period. A brief overview of

15

the impact of AIDS in the world, with particular emphasis on Africa is presented next.

The Impact of AIDS

AIDS is the leading cause of death in many countries in Africa. AIDS is reducing

investments in all sectors of African development especially in education. Many school teachers

and students are dying of AIDS. Students are also leaving school to take care of sick parents

who are too weak to care for themselves. Severely hard hit are young girls whose education is

sacrificed in these times of immense poverty created by AIDS as a result of parents' inability to

work. For example, UNAIDS (1998) reported that more than 30 percent of teachers in Malawi

and Zambia were HIV positive.

According to the World Bank (1999a), sub-Saharan African countries invest more than

50 per cent of their gross domestic product (GDP) in education. Deaths due to AIDS result in

negative returns on this investment in education. HIV/AIDS further challenges the quality of life

of people and puts pressure on governments to meet this challenge. Since human capital

development is desperately needed in Africa, attempts at preventing further deterioration in

education and capacity building will be welcomed by governments in the region.

Agriculture is the largest industry in the region both formal and informal (Hope, 1999).

Agriculture offers employment and provides the raw material for many industries. African

countries depend on agriculture to earn foreign exchange by exporting raw materials to foreign

markets. In return, capital goods such as machinery are imported for development projects like

roads, hospitals, industries, and manufacturing establishments. Deaths due to AIDS tend to

reverse this trend by lowering production resulting in less foreign exchange earnings.

As a result of this imbalance, major sectors of the economy that depend on technical

inputs from abroad are negatively impacted, especially health care (machinery, equipment, and

16

pharmaceuticals). Low agricultural production has led to poor nutrition of African households. In

addition, low production has also affected family income and budgets resulting in immeasurable

suffering to people (Bollinger & Antwi, 1999).

At the individual level, AIDS deaths lead to poor health of surviving family members.

This is because adults who suffer from AIDS tend to be the breadwinners in their families

(Topouzis, 1998). For example, social problems created by an increased orphan population leads

to untold hardships with concomitant repercussions for health and education of young adults.

AIDS related illness and subsequent deaths in Africa also impact worker productivity. Due to

absenteeism, expenditures such as hospital insurance and medical bills are increased, whereas

productivity is reduced (Decosas & Adrien, 1999). Health care provisions are overtaxed beyond

capacity as most African countries have limited health care facilities.

The prevalence of AIDS has further exacerbated the already precarious health

infrastructure systems in Africa (UNAIDS, 2005a). For example, in Ivory Coast and Zimbabwe,

HIV infected patients tend to occupy 50 to 80 percent of available hospital beds. In Cameroon, it

is not uncommon to find AIDS patients in hospitals without beds. The World Bank (1999a)

reported that treating an HIV patient for one year is equivalent to educating 10 primary school

children for one year in Africa. Due to the high cost of treatment some African governments

have constantly ignored the problem. However, the age of denial is over as the harsh realities of

HIV/AIDS continue to hunt political leaders all over Africa. Moreover, citizens suffering from

the disease continue to call on governments to accept the prevalence of HIV/AIDS and to design

programs to slow the devastation of the disease.

HIV/AIDS in Africa

Twenty years ago, Africa was relatively unscathed by the devastation of AIDS. The situation is much different today. According to UNAIDS (2005a), Africa is the leading epicenter of HIV/AIDS. Seventy percent (28.5 million) of people living with HIV/AIDS live in Africa. In 2005, 3.5 million new infections were reported and 11 million children were orphaned during the same period. The factors for the rapid spread of the disease are reported to be poverty, gender inequality, ignorance, and cultural practices (Anarfi, 1993; Awusabo-Asare, & Anarfi, 1997; Caldwell, 2000; Feldman, 1990; Mann, Tarantola, & Netter, 1996).

According to UNAIDS (2005a), in Botswana prevalence rates for pregnant women peaked from 38.5 percent in 1997 to 44.5 percent in 2001. In Zimbabwe similar high prevalence rates were reported for pregnant women. In 1997, a 29 percent rate was reported for Zimbabwe and this figure climbed to 35 percent in 2001. The most affected are the most productive adults between 15 to 45 year olds.

New infections continue to occur in Africa at alarming rates according to UNAIDS (2005a). Prevalence rates have surpassed the five percent watershed mark for all countries in the region. In effect, Africa has an explosive AIDS situation that warrants a vigorous innovative prevention approach. However, attempts in the past have not been very helpful at curtailing the severity and devastation of AIDS.

The most chilling impact of the disease is the reported drop in life expectancy from 62 years to 47 years for most countries in Africa. This shows an obvious decline in societal development (World Bank, 1999b). It is projected that 68 million people in the region will die of AIDS by the year 2025.

18

Declines in school enrollments have been reported in South Africa and Central African Republic. For example, a 20 percent drop in recent school enrollment in South Africa has been attributed to HIV/AIDS (UNAIDS, 2005a). The situation of HIV/AIDS in one such African country is examined in detail in the next section.

HIV/AIDS in Ghana

Ghana is situated on the west coast of Africa. Ghana is bordered to the west by Ivory Coast, to the east by Togo, and to the north by Burkina-Faso. On the southern shores is the Atlantic Ocean, making for a beautiful marine life. Climatic conditions are predominantly tropical with high temperatures exceeding 90 degrees during the summer (see map of Ghana in Figure 1). Ghana is a former British colony that attained political independence in 1957. There are 10 regions, with each region further divided into districts for local government purposes. Ghana's population as of 2000 is about 18.8 million (UNDP, 2000) and the gross domestic product (GDP) is $34 million, with a per capita income of $390.00. Agriculture, mining, and fishing are principal activities.

Ghana has a 15 percent inflation rate and is a member of the Highly Indebted Principal Countries (HIPC) of the world. Poverty abounds everywhere not only at the macro level but at the individual level. In 1997 the government introduced a "cash and carry" health delivery system. With this system, healthcare is provided for "cash payments" with no chance to use differed payments or insurance. According to the United Nations Development Program (UNDP, 1997), the introduction of user fees has resulted in delays in seeking treatment and an increased reliance on alternative health care facilities. This system has further alienated majority of Ghanaians with fewer having access to appropriate healthcare, as for example HIV/AIDS care. Ghana embraces numerous peoples and cultures.

19

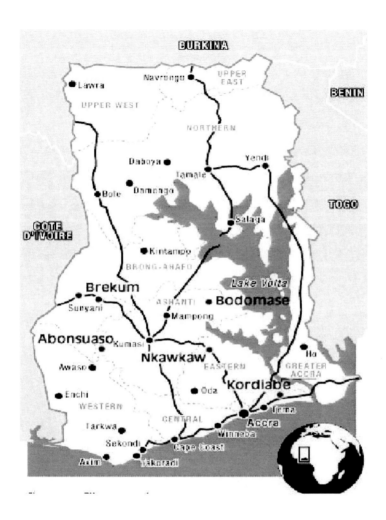

Figure 1. Map of Ghana

Note. From http://www.volu.org/map.html

According to UNDP (2000) Ghana's adult literacy rate is 54 percent with female

constituting a mere 38 percent and males about 62 percent. Fertility rate was 4.5 percent for 1999

with infant mortality rate at 63 per 1000 live births. Child mortality rate was 186 per 1000, and

general mortality rate (crude) was 10 per 1000.

In 1999, UNDP reported that public expenditure on health, as a percentage of Gross

Domestic Product (GDP) was 1.8 percent. This is alarming for it clearly shows that the

government spends very little on health. In addition, Mill and Anarfi (2002) reported that

poverty, societal beliefs, and poor education compromised the health of Ghanaians and made

them vulnerable to HIV infection.

Since 1986, various educational initiatives by the government and international

organizations in partnership with Ghanaians have attempted to educate people about the disease

so as to prevent further spread. This has not been successful as sero-prevalence rates continue to

increase among Ghanaian adults (UNAIDS, 2005a). HIV/AIDS is a major threat to government's

efforts at providing good health care services and maintaining the supply of human capital for

development in areas such as education, food, and agricultural production. It is urgent now more

than ever to stop the spread of HIV/AIDS because of the projected losses of human lives, the low

levels of life expectancy, human suffering, and the high populations of orphans for which

resources of the government and civil society organizations cannot cater for both in the short

term and the long term.

UNAIDS (2005b) estimated that the HIV prevalence rate for Ghana was above the five

percent watershed mark. Like other African countries with acute cases of AIDS, similar patterns

of spread appear to have emerged. For example, more women than men are infected and

especially hard hit are young adults (men and women) in the age cohort of 15 to 44 years old.

21

According to the Ghana AIDS Commission (2003) since 2001, over 200 people have been infected daily. In addition, 400,000 Ghanaians are reportedly living with HIV/AIDS with a projected doubling of this figure by the year 2005.

Perhaps the most disturbing feature of HIV/AIDS in Ghana is that it is more prevalent among the adult population of 15 to 45 year olds (the most productive of the population). Newspaper reports on HIV/AIDS since the beginning of year 2005 have warned of disaster if efforts are not intensified by the government to curb new cases of HIV infection (Ghana Press, 2005). Hardly a day passes without a feature on the disease and the need for action to slow the spread of the virus.

Data on economic impact of HIV/AIDS in Ghana are limited. However, the potential impact on other sectors of the economy including agriculture, households, and businesses in other countries in Africa appear to hold true for Ghana. Reports from severely affected countries indicate that HIV/AIDS increases health care cost especially provision of AIDS related care (UNAIDS, 2005a). Labor productivity is also slowed by the impact of AIDS due to absenteeism and deaths.

AIDS deaths may affect education in Ghana in three main ways: 1) the supply of teachers will be reduced, 2) children may be kept out of school to attend to dying parents and to work in subsistence agriculture where parents can no longer work, further depleting the already low school attendance in Ghana, and 3) low or poor returns on investment in education. When the younger adult population succumbs to AIDS, years spent in school for training and developments are lost.

Even though responses to the AIDS epidemic are varied, it is safe to categorize current approaches as medical or non-medical. It should also be noted that these responses are not

22

mutually exclusive as either approach may compliment each other. Many experts agree that

AIDS should be prevented, but there is no unanimity about how this is to be done. This study

examined how adults learned to change their sexual practices in response to the HIV/AIDS crises

in Ghana.

Operationally, AIDS education may be described as purposefully designed instruction

aimed at preventing HIV infection and the provision of information for managing AIDS resulting

in behavior change. This may include information about safer sex practices such as condom use,

fidelity, and abstinence that may lead to change in behavior. This type of education may be

carried out in school or out of school or both with the community as the ultimate beneficiary of a

healthy society.

Education is the most effective method of informing people about the disease and in

persuading people to adopt safer sex practices (Archie-Booker, 1996; DiClemente, 1996;

Sessions, 1998) but how adults learn to make changes in their sexual practices has received little

attention since the advent of HIV/AIDS.

Specifically this study examined how Ghanaian adults learned to make changes in their

sexual practices in response to HIV/AIDS. Health educators in the west have modeled their

practices on theoretical learning models of health behavior change. These theoretical frameworks

helped explain how people learned to make changes in their health behavior. Some of these

models were examined in detail to situate current work in the area of AIDS education and

behavior change that directly informed this study. Most of these models have been applied to

AIDS education in Africa (Awusabo-Asare & Anarfi, 1999; Awusabo-Asare, 1995; Bosompra,

1998).

Health Behavior Change Models

The Health Belief Model (HBM)

This is the most commonly used model to predict and explain individual health

behaviors. It states that health behavior is a function of the individual's perception and

interaction of threat or susceptibility to and severity of illness (Hochbuam, 1958; Janz & Becker,

1984; Rosentstock, Strecher, & Becker, 1994). The main purpose of the Health Belief Model

(HBM) is to explain behavior in terms of certain belief patterns. According to the model, a

person's motivation to undertake a health behavior can be divided into three main categories: 1)

Individual perception, 2) modifying behaviors, and 3) likelihood of action. Individual

perceptions are factors that affect the perception of illness. They deal with the importance of

health to the individual that is perceived susceptibility and perceived severity.

Modifying factors include demographic variables of perceived threat and cue to action.

Accordingly, the likelihood of action (learning to change behavior) is the result of perceived

susceptibility and severity of threat of disease condition. Thus, once an individual perceives a

threat to health and is cued to action, and perceives benefits to outweigh barriers then, the

individual most likely will undertake the recommended health behavior (McCormack, 1999).

A major criticism of the model is that factors other than health beliefs also influence

health behavior. The utility of the HBM in predicting HIV risk-reduction behaviors have been

inconsistent (Petosa & Jackson, 1991). Some studies have reported no relationship between the

two variables of susceptibility and severity (Brown, DiClemente & Reynolds, 1992), whereas

other studies have reported contradictory effects of perceived susceptibility and health behavior

(Aspinwall, Kemeny, Taylor, Schneider & Dudley, 1991).

24

Even the updated HBM with the inclusion of self-efficacy is reported to have several shortcomings. This includes the inability of the HBM to address the influence of culture, class, economics, environment, and life experience in shaping health behaviors. For example, what role poverty and ethnicity may play in HIV/AIDS infection has not been investigated. It also fails to consider the role of both habit and social network on learning and health behavior decisions and does not provide avenues for motivation for behavioral change (Siegal, 1990). The model is also silent on changed behavior maintenance, an important component of AIDS education.

Another limitation of the model is the fact that as a western developed model its constructs for eliciting health behavior are inconsistent with non-western societies. For example Adih and Alexander (1999) used modified constructs of the HBM and Social Learning Theory (STL) in Ghana and found that social factors not accounted for by the HBM and the SLT models were significant determinants of condom use (a risk reduction strategy) among Ghanaian adults. Also, it has been noted that health beliefs compete with an individual's other beliefs and attitudes, and can influence learning a new behavior (Campbell, 2001).

It may be argued that it is difficult to accurately measure health beliefs using quantitative behavior constructs. Since health beliefs are acquired over time, it is appropriate to employ a qualitative approach that may probe intricate personal beliefs that a questionnaire might fail to capture. For example, in Ghana people operate at two levels of health care. This includes traditional herbal practice that uses magic and herbs and the formal western healthcare system. This dualism is not accounted for by the HBM. Thus if one employs a research design that fails to capture this dichotomy, an accurate knowledge about health beliefs may not be obtained (Adih & Alexander, 1999).

The HBM does not address how health beliefs are formed nor changed, and the learning processes important for sexual behavior change. This explains why a qualitative paradigm may be more advantageous than other methods for probing intricate social behaviors such as sexual attitudes and beliefs.

In conclusion, it is important to note that the health belief model does not help us understand why the prevalence of HIV is so high, nor why and how people change health behaviors. This model is based on research that has used its theoretical frame discussed earlier as the basis for behavior change has failed to account for pertinent factors that predispose communities to the disease. The HBM appears to be insufficient as the basis for behavior change in the Ghanaian context, especially in understanding how Ghanaian adults make changes in their sexual practices in response to the HIV/AIDS crises.

Another health behavior model used by health educators is the theory of reasoned action. A brief overview is here presented.

The Theory of Reasoned Action (TRA)

This is a cognitive learning model that attempts to explain how people make health decisions. A major premise of the theory is that human beings are rational and they systematically process and weigh the result of their volitional health actions before they engage in one. TRA suggests that a person's behavior is determined by his/her intentions to perform the behavior and this intention is in turn a function of his/her attitude toward the behavior and his/her subjective norm (Ajzen & Fishbein, 1980). The theory maintains that three factors govern behavior performance (intention, attitude toward the behavior, and subjective norms).

Ajzen (1991) noted that intentions are "assumed to capture the motivational factors that influence a behavior, they are indications of how hard people are willing to exert, in order to perform the behavior" (p. 181). The TRA posits that health beliefs are important determinants of

an attitude whether negative or positive. Behavioral intentions may then lead to a health behavior

that is observable and under a person's volitional control. A person's attitude toward a behavior

is determined by a set of salient beliefs he/she holds about performing the behavior (subjective

and normative). Individual's behavioral intention is the most immediate factor influencing

behavior (Ajzen & Fisbein, 1980). The TRA has successfully been used to account for cigarette

and marijuana smoking cessation (Fishbein, 1982; Fisher, 1984). More recently it has been

applied to HIV/AIDS prevention.

A major criticism of this model is that it does not address the dynamic nature of behavior

and neglects relapse. In Ghana, rationality is a bargain and volitional control about health is an

essential commodity as these are dependent on social forces beyond the individual. Health

decisions are privy of government and family. In addition, customary practices bestow greater

powers about health decisions to males in the society. Thus women find it hard to make health

decisions that directly affect them. In this regard decisions about reproductive health such as the

number of children and the spacing of birth normally considered to be the privy of women due to

traditional beliefs have become contested issues (Awusabo-Asare, & Anarfi, 1997). Health

decisions are also determined by social status, economics, and the political climate according to

Anarfi (1993). One may ask why HIV/AIDS is prevalent among the poor in Ghana. The

assumption that humans are rational and make volitional decisions about sexual behavior and

hence risk factors and their avoidance according to Bosompra (1998) is not applicable in Ghana.

Again the construct of this model assumes that the individual will make rational decisions

for their own benefit. If this were true then we will expect everyone to make good choices about

sexual practices. On the contrary, this is not the case as behavior is a function of multiple factors

27

such as beliefs, customs, traditions, and knowledge.

The model also places emphasis on the individual, however, in non-western societies the group or community is more important than the individual. Due to these limitations, scientists turned to social learning theory for explanation about health behavior change.

Social Learning Theory (SLT)

Bandura (1977) proposed this model to explain human behavior. Using a three-way reciprocal theory in which personal factors (cognitive processes), behavior, and environmental influences continually interact in a process of reciprocal determinism. The theory holds that a person can shape the environment and can also be shaped by the environment. Therefore, change is bi-directional. In social modeling or observational learning, the participant observes someone else being reinforced for behaving in an appropriate or inappropriate manner (vicarious reinforcement).

According to Bandura (1986), self-efficacy is a major determinant of a person's effort to change behavior. A person can increase self-efficacy through personal persuasion such as receiving suggestions from others. This model has been applied to HIV/AIDS prevention messages. For example after Magic Johnson, a four time most valuable player (MVP) of the Los Angeles Lakers Basketball team announced his HIV status, many people adopted safer sex methods (Campbell, 2001).

Self-efficacy has been shown to be directly related to smoking cessation and goal attainment, but it is not clear whether related behaviors that require mastery of skills as for example, sexual practices, use of condoms or abstinence are sustained by self-efficacy. Though Bandura (1989) believes that self-efficacy is related to initiation of behaviors, it is not clear whether it is related to the maintenance of the intended behavior. Perhaps the processes involved

28

in making health decisions may illuminate our understanding of health behavior.

Wolf and Bond (2002) examined peer educators and AIDS-protective behavior in Ghana using (SLT) as a framework. They found interpersonal communication, gender, and ethnicity to be important factors for behavior change not accounted for by the constructs of the model. Thus, social factors influence sexual risk behaviors in Ghana. The importance of self-efficacy and the adoption of safer sex behavior remain largely unexplained. Another behavior change model applied to AIDS education is the consumer information-processing model. A brief overview is presented.

Consumer Information Processing Model (CIP)

Consumer Information Processing Model was developed by Bettman and McGuire (1979) to explain how consumers' process information they receive in the media. Like other models it was not developed specifically for health education but has been extensively applied to health behavior. There are two assumptions of the CIP. First, individuals are limited to how much information they can process and second, in order to increase the usability of information, individuals must combine little pieces of information into chunks for faster recall and use. Applied to HIV/AIDS education, CIP stipulates that the information must be available, be useful, and be in a friendly format. In addition, the most effective medium for communication must be chosen for the message.

The assumption is that an effective delivery medium will aid in information usage and recall. The model also assumes that information should be designed for a particular target audience and placed conveniently for their use. This has implications for non-western and non-literate societies. As already mentioned Ghana has over 42 local languages and only 5 are used for national broadcast on radio and television. The non-usage of a language on national television has implication for programs that use mass media channels for dissemination.

According to Bettman and McGuire (1979) information environment affects how easily people obtain, process, and use information. Thus this model stipulates that the location, format, readability and ability to process relevant information are essential for the adoption of healthy behavior. Since Ghana boasts many ethnic groups and languages, the challenge of this model will be the extent to which messages cater to people living with AIDS. This model underscores the importance of information and relevancy to match the level of comprehension. No studies were found in Ghana that specifically used this as its main investigative tool.

To understand the various changes people undertake so as to arrive at desired behavior change maintenance, and relapse avoidance, the stages of change model was examined.

The Stages of Change Model (SCM)

Prochaska and DiClemente (1983) proposed the Stages of Change or Trans-theoretical Model for behavior change. It evolved from smoking cessation research but has now been applied to other health conditions such as HIV/AIDS. This model views behavioral change as a process with individuals at different levels of the change continuum. It stipulates that since individuals are at different stages in the process, planned interventions should match their stage of readiness. The model comprises of six stages. The first is "pre-contemplation," during which the person may be unaware of the health problem or has not thought about change seriously. The second stage is called "contemplation" and is characterized by awareness and seriousness about change. The third stage is "preparation" and is dominated by planning action and making final adjustments before changing behavior. Stage four is dubbed the "action" stage. The individual implements some specific action plan to overtly modify behavior and environment. The fifth stage is "maintenance" during which desirable actions are continued so as to prevent relapse. The final stage is "termination" and it is at this stage that a zero temptation and ability to resist

relapse is cemented. An interesting aspect of this model is the fact that people can enter at any

stage and exit at any stage.

One limitation of this model however is the fact that people progress through these

changes whether they seek professional help or not. The critical issue to address therefore is how

to motivate people to change their sexual practices.

Based on the reviews of these behavior change models applied to AIDS education the

following conclusions can be drawn:

1. All models are based on western conception of disease and disease prevention, as

there appears to be more emphasis on the individual than the group.

2. Social factors such as ethnicity, language, customs, beliefs, and traditions are

important determinants of sexual practices and may influence decisions about

behavior change in response to HIV/AIDS.

3. These models provide inconclusive evidence about how adults learn to make

changes in their sexual practices.

Empirical Studies of HIV/AIDS in Ghana

The next section examined HIV/AIDS related non-medical studies in Ghana. Most of the

studies were conducted using university students as the principal sample. For example, Anarfi

(2000), Anarfi and Awusabo-Asare (1993) and Bosompra (1998) examined AIDS knowledge

among University of Ghana students. Bosompra (1998) examined condom use among university

students as a sexual behavior change strategy. Other studies were done comparing AIDS

knowledge among urban and rural folks (Anarfi & Antwi, 1995). One study examined migrant

workers, and commercial sex workers (Anarfi, 1993). In addition, health-seeking behaviors of people living with AIDS in Ghana were studied by Anarfi, Appiah, and Awusabo-Asare (1997).

Three studies were found that examined AIDS education from the perspective of the media

McCombie and Anarfi (1992), McCombie, Hornik, and Anarfi (2002) and Panford et al., (2001).

Anarfi (2000) in a study of university students and HIV/AIDS noted the lack of response

to HIV/AIDS by the administrators of the University of Ghana. The knowledge attitudes, and

behavior profile (KABP) questionnaire was used to determine knowledge, attitudes, and beliefs

about HIV/AIDS. Even though most students reported knowing other students living with

HIV/AIDS, university administrators denied knowledge of any student with HIV. Consequently,

Anarfi (2000) noted that this denial about the presence of HIV/AIDS is a reflection of what

exists in the country as a whole. So if the premier University of Ghana does not have any kind of

educational programs in place about HIV/AIDS, how can communities with less resources and

low levels of literacy be expected to know about the epidemic and consequently change their

sexual practices in response? The most disturbing aspect of HIV/AIDS in Ghanaian universities

is not only the lack of programs about AIDS, but the lack of being open about the presence of the

disease. Perhaps universities as places of teaching and research should take the lead in helping

people understand HIV/AIDS in non-western societies, as was the case in the west.

Similarly, Bosompra (1998) in a study of University of Ghana students on condom use

found that awareness of HIV/AIDS did not translate into increased condom use. Again, if

students were supposed to know better by adopting appropriate behaviors in the age of the AIDS

epidemic one would have expected an increased usage of condoms amongst university students.

The use of a quantitative questionnaire did not reveal much about sexual practices in Ghana.

Consequently, a qualitative interview would have yielded more of the personal nature of

HIV/AIDS in my view because of the cultural practices about sexual behavior that is secretive.

32

In probing a difficult area such as sexual behaviors, an in-depth qualitative interview will be more useful in understanding people's attitudes about sexual behaviors and the factors that put people at risk.

Anarfi (1993) in a study of 1147 adults representing all segments of Ghanaian population found that 93 percent were aware of AIDS and 80 percent knew about condoms. However, condom use was low, 20 percent according to Bosompra (1998), and inconsistent. Less than half of the sample believed that condoms could protect them against HIV infection. The researcher failed to identify the educational or literacy levels of participants. This would have been helpful given the low literacy levels among rural dwellers. Anarfi (2000) reported that religion, faithfulness, and culture were the principal reasons for not practicing safer sex methods in Ghana but the researcher failed to substantiate this assertion.

Given the already low literacy rates for Ghana (40 percent according to UNDP, 1999) perhaps understanding the relationship between educational level and AIDS related behavior change would have been beneficial. Previous studies have already established the presence of HIV/AIDS in Ghana and there is no need to investigate this further. What is important is why the prevalence rate for Ghana continues to mount in spite of numerous educational efforts. In particular, it would have been helpful to know how adults learn to make changes in their sexual practices in response to the HIV/AIDS crisis.

Anarfi and Antwi (1995) in a study of two urban areas in Ghana found that although many respondents claimed to have changed their behavior since the outbreak of HIV/AIDS, based on education provided by the National AIDS Control Program (NACP) (Radio, television, billboard, pamphlet, and public service announcements). Only a small percentage reported condom use. Though they hypothesized that increased condom use was positively related to increased awareness about risk factors, this was not supported by the findings. They concluded

that respondents had not actually incorporated the educational messages they received. They,

however, failed to examine the factors for this discrepancy. An understanding of the factors that

promote or deter people from adopting healthy behaviors is crucial for slowing the epidemic.

Bosompra (1989) in an evaluation of an AIDS education project undertaken by the

Ministry of Health (MOH) found that drama on AIDS related themes led to increased levels of

knowledge about HIV/AIDS and motivated both rural and urban audiences to change their

sexual behaviors. But no evidence was presented to help other researchers understand how adults

initiated and maintained these changes in sexual practices. This study strived to understand how

Ghanaian adults made changes in their sexual practices in response to the HIV/AIDS crisis.

Awusabo-Asare and Anarfi (1999) in a study on health seeking behaviors of people

living with AIDS (PLWA) found that traditional healers and spiritualists were among the most

important healthcare outlets in Ghana. They concluded that this was the case because many

people believed the origin and mode of transmissions of HIV to be due to supernatural forces.

Probably, Ghanaians use traditional herbalists and spiritualists because they have been the most

accessible care providers over the years. Even though this finding should have prompted the

researchers to examine how Ghanaians learn about HIV/AIDS and the factors that influence

them to choose traditional healers, this was not examined.

Awusabo-Asare and Anarfi (1999a) proposed a proximate determinant framework for

analyzing routes to HIV infection and intervention in Ghana. The model attempts to bring

together the remote and the proximate factors responsible for risk taking behavior and

subsequent infection. Accordingly, the researchers believe that intervention strategies should

tackle both causes and their manifestations. Whereas this proposal is well founded, the

34

researchers failed to discuss methods as to how this could be accomplished and missed an

opportunity to examine learning with respect to sexual practices in response to HIV/AIDS in

Ghana.

The few empirical studies available on HIV/AIDS (Anarfi, 2000; Awusabo-Asare &

Anarfi, 1999; Bosompra, 1998; McCombie & Anarfi, 1992; Mill & Anarfi, 2002) in Ghana have

failed to examine HIV/AIDS from the perspective of changes in sexual practices, a key

component in understanding how HIV/AIDS could be eradicated. This study fills that void in the

literature. Even though all researchers alluded to the importance of social factors for behavior

change, no one specifically examined how these interplay in the fight against AIDS.

No study in Ghana specifically examined AIDS education for Ghanaian adults. For

example, Awusabo-Asare and Anarfi (1999) merely examined proximate determinants of

HIV/AIDS in Ghana. The principal research designs used were quantitative methods to

determine behavior adaptations in Ghana. As noted earlier Ghana has a high illiteracy rate

among adults but none of these studies explained how they accounted for this problem. In

addition, all of these studies used quantitative approaches and failed to capture people's stories

about diseases and health crisis. To this end, I used a qualitative research paradigm believing that

this helped to better understand the process of change experienced by participants.

The intricacies involved in sexual behavior change adaptation demands that various

cultural factors be examined. One way of ensuring adoption of behavior change is audience

knowledge and relevancy of information to the audience (Atkin & Rice, 2001; Elder, 2001;

Hornik, 2002) and the medium through which the message is adequately conveyed to recipients.

The next section examines attempts at mass media educational initiatives and their potential for

changes in sexual practices.

Mass Media and Behavior Change

Health communication is the systematic attempt to positively influence the health

practices of large populations. The primary goal of "health communication is to bring about

improvement in health related practices and in turn health status" (Graeff, Elder & Mills Booth,

1993, p.13). Health communication according to Graeff et al., (1993) has had a significant role in

changing child survival in areas of diarrhea disease control and immunization in a variety of

cultural settings in Africa.

The Centers for Disease Control and Prevention (CDC, 1995) defined health

communication as a multidisciplinary theory-based practice designed to influence the

knowledge, attitudes, beliefs, and behaviors of individuals and communities. Thus a

communication program is the delivery of planned messages through one or more channels to

target audiences through the use of materials. Successful information programs should share a

number of basic characteristics which include: 1) activities planned to fit the community and

target audiences needs and wants, 2) a variety of activities including mass media that can be

directed over a period of time to the target audience, 3) a measurable program objective, 4) a

commitment to evaluation by tracking and measuring progress toward objectives, and 5) the

efficient use of people and other resources.

Panford, Nyaney, Amoah Opoku, and Garbrah Aidoo (2001) examined the use of folk

media in HIV/AIDS prevention in rural Ghana with the use of radio. They designed AIDS

information based on the cultural practices of the people based on the local language, methods of

information dissemination, and delivered the message over the local radio.

Ansu-Kyeremeh cited in Panford et al. (2001) defines folk media as:

Any form of endogenous communication system which by virtue of its origin from and

36

integration in to a specific culture serves as a channel for messages in a way and manner

that requires the utilization of the values, symbols, institutions and ethos of the host

culture through its unique qualities and attributes. Folk media are often used for personal

as well as group information sharing and discussion and draw their popularity from their

entertaining nature. (p. 1560)

Types of folk media include storytelling, puppetry, proverbs, visual art, drama, role play,

concerts, gong beating, dirges, songs, drumming and dancing. Panford et al. (2001) observed that

since folk media was based on local customs and practices it had a greater potential for affecting

behavior change among rural people with little or no education. "The power of folk media in

changing behaviors in rural Africa results mainly from the media's originality and the audience's

trust in the source of the messages which often comes from people real to their audience"

(Panford et al., 2001, p. 1560). Panford et al. (2001) found that audience trust of the source of

the message was instrumental in making decisions about sexual practices and behavior change.

In addition they found that media messages that were based on traditional practices (language,

drums, local theatre) had a greater potential for the adoption of changed behaviors. Panford et al.

(2001) used folk media to refer largely to dissemination of health information in a local language

over the radio. Since media is a major component of AIDS education in Ghana, these findings

have important ramifications for learning in adulthood.

Mass Media in Ghana

There are over 40 radio stations and four television channels in Ghana. With reference to

print media, there are over 50 registered newspapers and magazines in Ghana. The Ghana

government owns and operates two major television stations and the Malaysian government in

partnership with private Ghanaian companies operates two television channels. The largest

37

circulating newspapers are state owned and operated. Though there over 40 languages that are

spoken in Ghana, only Akan, Dagbani, Ewe, Ga, Hausa, and Nzima are used for program

transmission on radio. There is no critical dialogue on issues that affect people who are suffering

from HIV/AIDS in the media because of stakeholder interests that may be at variance with

government policy on HIV/AIDS. This has created a situation where the government has no

control on the purpose and type of HIV/AIDS prevention education that people receive from the

mass media. The principle of the government is to provide as much information as possible in

the hope that it would somehow make an impact on the people. This explains why awareness

about HIV/AIDS is high but changes in sexual practices are very low.

In an evaluation of AIDS awareness campaigns in Ghana, McCombie and Anarfi (1992)

and McCombie, Hornik, and Anarfi (2001) found that ten months after a nationwide mass media

campaign, there had been a significant increase in levels of awareness of AIDS among adults but

this was not reflected in behaviors consistent with safer sex practices. Respondents reported

multiple sexual partners, polygamy, and low levels of condom usage. There appeared to have

been a disjoint between what the people were hearing and the expectation of planners.

Even though the expectation was adoption of safer sex practices, this was not achieved.

Perhaps the channels of communications were inconsistent with traditional methods of message

delivery. Therefore, there is a missing link between mass media health promotion campaigns and

the adoption of behavior change. McCombie and Anarfi (1992) failed to discuss the factors for

these discrepancies in their research findings. This study examined how Ghanaian adults made

changes in their sexual practices in response to the HIV/AIDS crisis.

Mill and Anarfi (2002) in a qualitative study of HIV risk environment for Ghanaian

women found that large-scale media educational programs on HIV prevention were ineffective.

38

However, the researchers did not give reasons for this conclusion. It would have been beneficial

to AIDS educators if factors for these failures in their view were delineated. In contrast this study

examined how Ghanaian adults learned to make changes in their sexual practices in response to

the AIDS epidemic.

Though Mill and Anarfi (2002) acknowledged the prospective role of traditional rulers

and healers in the dissemination of information about HIV/AIDS, they failed to examine the

context and type of learning associated with HIV/AIDS in Ghana. It is my belief that this study

fills that void.

Qualitative research paradigm allows the researcher to probe details, especially issues

germane to participants such as coping strategies and behavior change adaptation strategies.

Though Mill and Anarfi (2002) employed this tool in their investigation of Ghanaians they failed

to examine in detail why HIV sero-prevalence is on the rise in Ghana.

Kelly (1995) stated that if communities could organize readily and effectively on their

own against HIV and other social health problems they would have already done so. However,

the communities most vulnerable to HIV are often those with many other competing social

problems, with limited political and resource support, and without the strong infrastructure

needed to launch and maintain wide-scale sustained HIV primary prevention efforts. This

underscores the importance of how individuals and communities make changes in their sexual

practices.

Hornik (2002) argues that there are three complementary models of behavior change

implicit in public health communication campaigns: 1) the first model assumes that individual

exposure to the message affects individual behavior, 2) the second model characterized as the

social diffusion model focuses on process of change in public norms which leads to behavior change among social groups and, 3) the third model deals with institutional and organizational changes at the policy level that eventually affect behavior.

Accordingly, Hornik (2002) believes that smoking and sexual behaviors will change only when social norms change. Changing social norms in non-western societies require culture change, and this becomes a cardinal goal of educators and government with respect to HIV/AIDS. This assertion is important because African countries are so culturally engrained that a change in individual behavior requires a corresponding societal norm change. For example, a change in individual sexual practices requires a corresponding societal change in perception about polygamy and other cultural practices.

Backer, Rogers, and Sopory (1992) believe that health communication campaigns can help health behavior change. They found that television, radio, film, and print media are increasingly being used to present health information and stimulate awareness, attitude change, and behavior change. For example, the most successful and best-documented health behavior change campaigns in the west with significant mass media components are the North Karelia Project in Finland and the Stanford Heart Campaign in California (Backer et al., 1992).

In 1972, Finland realized it had the world's highest death rates from cardiovascular disease. North Karelia, a region in Finland, had the highest rates within the country. The North Karelia Project was designed as a community wide project to carry out a comprehensive behavior change education. Key personnel were enlisted not only in the health sector but also in agriculture, sports, and education. Information campaigns were designed that used extensive mass media such as leaflets, posters, radio, and television. In addition, direct means of intervention such as health meetings with schools, community centers, and work places. Community leaders were enlisted as project assistants and to explain media messages to people.

40

Over the years numerous studies have reported significant drops in cholesterol levels and the prevalence of high blood pressure than the rest of Finland. Implicit in health communication and behavior change is the process of learning in adulthood. This study examined in detail how Ghanaian adults learned to make changes in their sexual practices in response to HIV/AIDS.

Chapter Summary

This literature review has given us an overview of HIV/AIDS education. It has outlined the prevalence and the quest for solution to the problem of AIDS in the world and in particular Africa. Further it has focused on Ghana where at the micro level, the problem is more intense than the rest of the world. Education to prevent transmission has been used to address the problem not only in Ghana but the rest of the world.

These educational efforts have followed some model of learning and behavior change adoption such as the health belief model, the social learning theory, the theory of reasoned action, the consumer information processing model and the stages of change model of behavior change. The utility of the health belief model in predicting health behavior change has been inconsistent over the years according to Petosa and Jackson (1991). Other factors not accounted for by the health belief model, such as demographic and cultural factors, also influence health behavior change.

The theory of reasoned action assumes that human beings are rational and systematically process and weigh the results of their volitional health decisions. The theory of reasoned action suggests that a person's behavior is determined by an intention that in turn is a function of the individual's subjective norms. However, we know that volitional control about health decisions is influenced by many factors not accounted for by the theory.

Though social learning theory offers some promise about effecting health behavior change, it also fails to account for pertinent social factors important for behavior change in Ghana according to Wolf and Bond (2002). However, one model that offers a beacon of hope for health educators is the consumer information processing model. This model addresses the environment, the information channels, and the readability and usability of available health information. This model addresses the environment of the recipient of health information. In addition, this model also stipulates that the most effective medium for communication must be used to enhance behavior change adoption. Since Ghana uses mass media to deliver its AIDS education, this model underscores the importance of information delivery, channels of communication, and relevancy of the information to match the level of comprehension of recipients of the information.

As reviewed above some studies of educational efforts that have been undertaken in Ghana but these studies failed to further illuminate our understanding of Ghanaian sexual practices in the era of HIV/AIDS. As a result of this inadequacy and the determination to stop the spread of HIV/AIDS, I examined how Ghanaian adults made changes in their sexual practices in response to the HIV/AIDS crisis.

CHAPTER THREE

METHODOLOGY

Introduction

This chapter presents an overview of the research methodology that this study employed

in examining how Ghanaian adults changed their sexual practices in response to the HIV/AIDS

crisis. The four questions examined in this study were:

1. What changes have Ghanaian adults made in their sexual practices since learning

   about HIV/AIDS?

2. How do Ghanaian adults learn (formal or informal) what they need to know to make

   changes in their sexual practices in response to the HIV/AIDS crisis?

3. What is the learning process that leads Ghanaian adults to change their sexual

   practices in response to the HIV/AIDS crisis?

4. What factors encourage or deter Ghanaian adults from making changes in their sexual

   practices in response to the HIV/AIDS crises?

This chapter describes the methodology for this study under the following headings: 1)

the design of the study, 2) sample selection, 3) data collection, 4) data analysis, 5)

validity/reliability, and 6) researcher biases.

Research Design

This study employed the tools of a basic qualitative design (Merriam, 1998). According

to Merriam (1998), the term basic or generic qualitative study refers to studies that exemplify the

43

characteristics of qualitative research by drawing from concepts, models, and theories in other

areas of study such as psychology and sociology. In basic qualitative studies data are collected

through interviews, observations or document analysis and the analysis usually results in

identification of recurrent patterns such as factors or categories and a description of these

patterns. The essence of this study was to understand how Ghanaian adults learned to change

their sexual practices in response to the HIV/AIDS crisis. In addition, the goal of this study was

to describe this change process by adults who had made changes in their sexual practices since

learning about HIV/AIDS. Thus, this study used the tools of the generic qualitative methodology

as explained in data collection, analysis, and presentation of findings.

This investigation identified factors that affected the adoption of changed sexual practices

over time. HIV/AIDS is more prevalent in less endowed communities especially adults, women,

and the ethnically disenfranchised. It is expected that the identification of the factors for behavior

change will lead to effective education about HIV/AIDS that is based on culture of the affected

community. By studying the narratives of people who have made changes in their sexual

practices, I hoped to understand why people make changes in sexual practices and why some

people do not. Perhaps by identifying the factors that encouraged or deterred behavior change,

adult educators would be able to facilitate more appropriate curricula designs for AIDS

education in Ghana.

One feature of the qualitative method is that it allows in-depth study of a particular site

over a period of time (Merriam, 1998).This means that the local community will be engaged as

co-constructors of knowledge as well as principal informants for the study. The meanings they

attach to their practices become important to the researcher in the analysis of data. Members of

the community did help the researcher understand what needed to be done to change the

44

troubling situation HIV/AIDS from their perspectives.

HIV/AIDS education is about changing individuals and community perceptions about the disease. In this regard, input from the community is important. I solicited the help of members of a Ghanaian community who had experience with HIV/AIDS to give their input as co-constructors of knowledge.

AIDS is a unique phenomenon to educators because of the personal nature of the problem. HIV/AIDS challenges educators in how sex education is taught in schools. In the community, AIDS presents special problems for educators in how to change age-old cultural assumptions about sex and sexual practices.

Equally important is the ability of educators to understand the setting so as to design preventive educational programs. In this regard, this study as explained by Patton (1990) was best suited to the qualitative methodology, because of the goal to understand the context of the problem. For example, since the early 1990s there have been numerous attempts to educate Ghanaian adults about the problem, but the prevalence rates continue to rise. In line with Patton's (1990) assertion, this analysis strived for depth of understanding of the extenuating circumstances of AIDS and education about AIDS. Specifically, how change in sexual practices were initiated, carried out, and maintained over time. The factor(s) that encouraged or hindered the adoption of changed sexual practices are critical for future instructions on HIV/AIDS.

The Ghana AIDS Commission and other agencies engaged in AIDS education use many formats to deliver their educational program, as for example, radio, television, pamphlets, billboards and public service announcements. These mass media methods are good at reaching large audiences (McCombie & Anarfi, 1993; McCombie, Hornik & Anarfi, 2002). However, it has not been determined just how people use the information they received to change behaviors

45

especially behaviors that place people at risk for HIV/AIDS. Research on HIV/AIDS in Ghana

has not gone far enough in providing avenues for people to express to their feelings and emotions

on HIV/AIDS. For example, the use of quantitative methods by Anarfi (1993, 1995, 1996, 1998,

Hornik & Anarfi, 2002), Awusabo-Asare (1997), McCombie and Anarfi (1993) through

structured questionnaires failed to provide ample opportunity for members of the communities

affected to voice their position on HIV and AIDS education. With reference to Anarfi's (2000)

study of University of Ghana students, even though students expressed knowledge about HIV

they still harbored negative feelings against those living with HIV in a hypothetical question

when asked if they will share a room with an HIV positive student.

Bosompra (1998) acknowledged that the use of the structured interview format failed to

capture the emotions and feelings of the nature of AIDS amongst students who knew people

ailing with AIDS. In order to correct this shortcoming in previous research, I used the qualitative

method, whereby through the use of semi-structured interviews I dialogued with people directly

involved in changes in sexual practices.

Qualitative procedures are "ideal for phenomena about which there is little certain

knowledge" (Krathwohl, 1998, p. 229). This is especially true in the case of HIV/AIDS Africa.

Qualitative procedures are also useful for exploration to find out how to understand phenomena

(Krathwohl, 1998). This is particularly important for Ghana where there still is a struggle to

understand HIV/AIDS. Due to ignorance on the part of traditional healers who claim to have a

"cure" for AIDS, the educational messages of both the government and non-governmental

organizations become a contested terrain between the government on one hand, and traditional

healers on the other hand, with the illiterate population the big losers.

46

Stake (1995) maintains that qualitative methods have several advantages among which are that the method helps humanize problems and data. For the use of the qualitative method uncovers the meanings and feelings of people that quantitative methods cannot do. By putting a human face on the issue, policy makers in Ghana may allocate more money for AIDS education.

Another advantage of this methodology is that it helps the investigator describe complex personal and interpersonal phenomena that would be impossible to portray with quantitative research single dimensional scales. This is very important because culturally, sexual practices are not discussed in the public domain in Ghana so one way of bringing to the open HIV/AIDS is an in-depth qualitative research interview. The openness of my conversations with participants demonstrated that they were happy to talk about HIV/AIDS and sexual practices.

In addition, the qualitative methodology for the study of AIDS education helped the investigator get an insider's view of sexual practices in Ghana that would otherwise be unavailable to the researcher. This was because of the development of trust and the fact that data sets were mediated through the researcher.

Due to the personal nature of AIDS, quantitative methods are unable to truly capture the emotional state of those dealing with the problem. However, qualitative methods, because they provide opportunities for face to face interactions of researcher and subjects, help to attach emotions and feelings to the phenomena, beliefs, behaviors, and coping skills. This makes it easier for policy makers to identify with people so as to provide the necessary assistance they might need. For example, sometimes the faces of HIV/AIDS patients and their accompanying personages, even their situation, context, and accompanying emotional and social climate and milieu could be a factor in how the Ghana government responds to this health and social crisis.

The qualitative method helps access problems without obvious starting places

(Krathwohl, 1998). This is critical for Ghana because of the increasing HIV/AIDS cases and the

urgency to "do something" immediately to slow the high prevalence in the country. Without an

obvious starting place a qualitative research design will help provide structure upon which to

base further studies. This makes the qualitative methodology very important for AIDS educators

and adult health educators in Ghana. Thus qualitative methods are most useful in situations

where research is lacking as the case is for Ghana in terms of HIV/AIDS education, or where the

problem involves complex interactivity (Krathwohl, 1998).

Several assumptions of the qualitative research paradigm guided this study. One is that

the researcher was principally interested more in the process than outcomes. My principal focus

was in understanding how Ghanaian adults made decisions about safer sex practices so as to

protect themselves against HIV/AIDS. In doing so how they learned about HIV/AIDS that

resulted in making changes in sexual practices became important.

The experiences of those being studied and the meanings they make of the life situations

are important. According to Merriam (1998), the key concern in qualitative research is in

understanding the phenomenon from the participants' perspective and not the researcher's

perspective. For example, my goal was to understand what meaning people ascribed to certain

behavior cultural practices that exposed Ghanaian adults to HIV prevalence. Specifically, since

my aim was to understand how Ghanaians learned to make changes in sexual practices, it was

important that the meanings they made of their learning resources were understood from their

perspectives (emic or insider perspectives according to Merriam, 1998).

The researcher is the primary instrument for data collection in qualitative research.

Merriam (1998) writes that data are mediated through the researcher rather than through some

48

inanimate inventory, questionnaire, or computer. For example, I wanted to be able to be responsive to questions that participants might have about current approaches to HIV/AIDS education in Ghana. Culturally, it is appropriate to interact both verbally and non-verbally with participants. This is of value to most illiterates who tend to be suspicious of questionnaires and other quantitative research instruments. In addition, sexual behavior, being a very sensitive area requires development of trust prior to an interview process. The qualitative research paradigm provides this opportunity for having in-depth knowledge of the participants. As the primary instrument for data collection, the researcher had the opportunity to make quick observations and interpretations where applicable. This ultimately helped in presenting a thick and rich final observation and report of the phenomenon.

Field notes are essential to the process of data collection and may actually help validate the process. This requires that the researcher must physically be at the site of the investigation in order to observe the phenomenon in the natural setting. I visited Ghana in the month of October, 2004 and interviewed participants, as well as observed what was being done to educate Ghanaians. I believe that my presence at the site helped me understand what was actually going on with the phenomenon of HIV/AIDS as it affected Ghanaian adults.

Sample

The goal of this study was to understand how Ghanaian adults learned to make changes in their sexual practices in response to the HIV/AIDS crisis. It was therefore important that Ghanaian adults, especially the group that made changes in their sexual practices in response to the AIDS crisis, be examined to find out how and at what point they made these changes. This information would guide HIV/AIDS educators' to better tailor educational messages to people dealing with the crisis. Thus, a purposive sampling strategy was employed in this study.

49

Sampling in field research involves the selection of a research site, time, people, or event (Burgess, 1982). There are two major types of sampling, namely, probability sampling and the non-probability sampling. Merriam (1998) writes that since generalizations from sample to the population are not the goal of qualitative research, the best type of sampling is non-probability sampling. I employed a purposive sampling strategy, a common method of non-probability sampling to select samples that I believe yielded rich results and answered my research questions.

Sampling Criteria

Three sampling criteria were employed in identifying participants for the study. First, adults engaged in community improvement of their neighborhood, and willing to participate in the study by consenting to be interviewed. Second, people who had changed at least one sexual practice in response to HIV/AIDS. The third selection criterion was gender. I strived to have a diversified pool of participants in order to understand learning about HIV/AIDS from the perspectives both women and men in the community. The map of Northern Ghana identifies the research site of Savelugu/Nanton District (see Figure 2, a map of Northern Region and the study location of Savelugu/Nanton District.).

The District map of Northern Ghana shows the location of Savelugu/Nanton, the study site. The map shows the proximity of Savelugu/Nanton to Burkina-Faso to the North, Ivory Coast to the west and Togo to the east. The map also shows the crossroads that leads to Savelugu/Nanton and situates Ghana within the West African region.

Transportation plays a vital role in the economic activities of the people of Savelugu/Nanton District. Truckers, market women, and peripatetic traders all come to trade in various wares in Savelugu/Nanton District. Due to its proximity to Tamale the regional capital,

50

Savelugu/Nanton enjoys the benefits of an urban center though still retaining a rural charm.

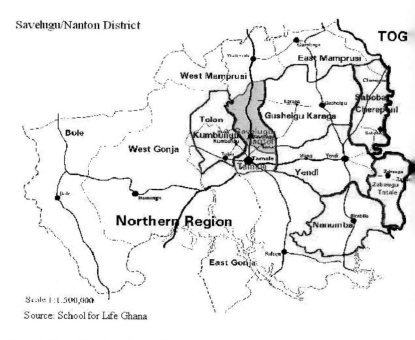

Figure 2. Map of Savelugu/Nanton District

Note. From http://www.ghanavenskabsgruppcrnc.dk/uk/sfl/tamale.html

---

The study was sited in Savelugu/Nanton because of its nearness to Tamale, the regional

capital of the Northern Region which is urban. Savelugu/Nanton is a mix of rural and urban areas

because of its proximity to Tamale, and the site provided opportunities to interrogate the

rural/urban divide in Ghana in terms of disease discourse. Secondly, Savelugu/Nanton is also a

travel stop for truckers to Burkina-Faso, Togo, and the Ivory Coast, then, the research site also provided a unique opportunity to understand crossroad culture, and dialogue about HIV/AIDS.

Upon my arrival in Tamale, Ghana, my informant helped me identify ten people who agreed to be interviewed for the study because they met the selection criteria. However, I also observed that these individuals were members of a self-help community group engaged in HIV/AIDS education as well as a forum for community improvement called Jarazama hereafter referred to as the group. Ten members of this group became the core sample for the study. My initial plan was to identify individuals using a snowballing sampling technique but this did not happen because my informant found this group that was readily available and willing to participate in this study. Furthermore, I had planned to include participants from rural and urban areas of Ghana so as to determine how accessible HIV/AIDS educational information was to people across the rural and urban divide because of illiteracy, but this did not occur in the field.

There are no records on the specific date the group was formed according to my informant. The informant said that during his college days he and a few friends who hail from the area decided to come together and strategize on issues affecting the community. Their goal was community improvement. However, with the advent of HIV/AIDS, and the fact that Savelugu/Nanton is situated on a major thoroughfare that links Ghana to neighboring Burkina-Faso to the North, and the Republic of Togo to the east, their focus shifted to prevention education about the new disease. This was because the area had been identified as a high prevalence area because of truck drivers, underground sex workers, and nearness to high prevalence Burkina-Faso, Togo, and the Ivory Coast.

My informant explained that there was no formal application for membership except the willingness to participate in the group's mission and goals of community improvement. To this end, membership was sometimes large and sometimes low. He observed that there was a surge in

52

membership because all principal actors in HIV/AIDS education (the government, and non-governmental organizations) continue to urge people to change their sexual practices because of increased prevalence rates for Ghana and high deaths rates for people with AIDS in Ghana.

In conjunction with the District Assembly, members of the group helped other community members understand the nature of the disease and the need to adopt safer sex practices. Members of the group carried out these educational activities through word of mouth, the use of resource persons, informal discussions, and distribution of literature on HIV/AIDS, such as posters, pamphlets, and condom demonstration. Another outlet where the group engaged the community was at traditional community gatherings like naming ceremonies, marriage ceremonies, festivals, and on traditional market days. At these gatherings members engaged their audience informally by explaining the need to adopt safer sex practices because of the disease.

This core group of people thus constituted the sample. My goal was to identify people with rich information that would help inform the research questions about what they learned about HIV/AIDS, how they learned and what factors encouraged or deterred them from making these important behavioral changes.

The sample included both men and women who had changed their sexual practices in order to have a more diversified sample for this study. This diverse sample provided me the opportunity to truly understand AIDS education in Ghana from the perspectives of the participants. Participants' names were disguised to protect their identity and confidentiality. In line with University of Georgia protocol on human subject research I asked for and gained access to this group through informed consent (see appendix A).

Data Collection

The term data refers to the rough materials researchers collect from the world they study. They are the particulars that form the basis of analysis (Bogdan & Biklen, 1998). Data includes recorded materials such as interview transcripts and researchers' observations, field notes, diaries, photographs, documents, and newspaper articles. According to Bogdan and Biklen (1998) data serve as the stubborn facts that save the writing you will do from unfounded speculation. Data grounds you to the empirical world and when rigorously collected, link qualitative research to other forms of science (Bogdan & Biklen, 1998).

Though several data collection techniques are available to the qualitative researcher, I employed the semi-structured interview method (see Appendix B for actual interview schedule). An interview is a purposeful conversation (Morgan, 1988). An interview is directed by one individual in order to get information from another individual (Bogdan & Biklen, 1992).The purpose of an interview in qualitative research is to gather descriptive data in the respondent's own words. The way respondents describe the phenomenon under investigation helps the researcher understand the perspectives of those respondents. "Good interviews produce rich data filled with words that reveal the respondents' perspectives" (Bogdan & Biklen, 1992, p. 97).

The Interview Process

I used an informal semi-structured interview format. I believe that a semi-structured interview protocol provided the guidelines that addressed the main questions about sexual practices in Ghana. The purpose was not to miss an important research question as well as not to waste time and money in the process. Interview questions were based on the research questions. To enable me to capture the voices of my respondents, I tape-recorded all my four sessions for easy transcription and analysis. I conducted three group interviews with all participants on three

54

different market days. These market days were weekly and were on Tuesday, Wednesday, and

Thursday while I was in Savelugu/Nanton. During each session I asked key questions about their

sexual practices, how they learned about HIV/AIDS for the first time, what they did after

learning about HIV/AIDS, and why they persisted when others did not.

My first interviews provided opportunities to refine my questioning strategies. I realized

The interviews were one on one with each participant but within the group setting. Each

interview lasted about 40 minutes. Each day's interview process spanned about four hours. Four

participants were interviewed on each market day. In addition, because the interviews were

conducted in the open and not in a closed space like an office, or building, some of the tape

recordings picked up background noise and had to be discarded for inaudibility and lack of

clarity for transcribing purposes.

My first interviews provided opportunities to refine my questioning strategies. I realized

that I interviewed only four participants in the span of the whole day. I also realized that I needed

to take more control of the interview process and to quickly follow up with probes after asking

major questions such as when participants first learned about HIV/AIDS. All the interviews were

conducted in a group but focused on one participant at a time.

My second interviews were again conducted on the following market day in the

community. By this time I was beginning to feel more at ease with my questioning skills and my

assertiveness in the process. I also realized that I could not control the background noise during

the process because members knew a lot of people in the community who were on their way to

the market and stopped by to greet participants. I was able to get four interviews done and was

also successful at reducing the background noise to a minimal level though not completely.

My third interviews followed the same pattern but were more relaxed and more probing.

During the third session I also reviewed my questions with them and had a discussion with them about what development projects they will like to see in their community. Surprisingly most of them said opportunities for jobs.

I also followed the group to a community where they conducted peer education and observed condom use demonstration. This provided a further opportunity to observe the group in action. I also attended one naming ceremony where members engaged attendees on safer sex education. I was allowed to take photographs of these educational activities of the group. I also kept a note book in which I recorded my observations as I conducted the interviews. This provided an opportunity to further probe areas that I felt I needed more information.

I also collected posters, pamphlets, and photographed billboards in Ghana on HIV/AIDS education. This constituted a second source of data. Document analysis is the practice of examining a set of documents that are used to support specific goals and objectives. This researcher was interested in examining how the documents used in AIDS education in Ghana (posters, billboards, pamphlets) related to the cultural practices of the people in the research area.

Data Analysis

Data analysis involves the organization of what an individual has seen, heard, and read so that he/she can make sense of what you have learned in the field or natural setting. Working with the data, one can describe, create explanations, pose hypothesis, develop theories, and link stories to other stories. According to Glesne (1999) one must categorize, synthesize, search for patterns, and interpret the data that have been collected. Data sources were analyzed using the constant comparative analytic method (Bogdan & Biklen, 1998). Merriam (1998) points out that the constant comparative method as a data analysis method was originally developed by Glaser and Strauss (1967) for grounded theory, but it has become a basic strategy used by all qualitative researchers who are not seeking to build a substantive theory as in grounded theory research.

56

Although this study was not a grounded theory research, I employed the constant

comparative method in my data analysis. First, when I returned to Athens, Georgia I transcribed

all the tapes according to the order in which I conducted the interviews. Second, based on my

research questions I coded all transcribed interviews. Third, I looked for themes in the coded

interviews based on preponderance of data according to the various research questions. This

approach was constant and consumed a lot of time as I kept buildings themes, and collapsing

some themes into other sub themes. This process, though time consuming, allowed me to refine

some of the themes. Finally, based on my codes and themes I was able to glean several findings

which are presented in the next chapter.

In addition, I collected documents comprising posters, pamphlets, and magazines that

stakeholders employed in HIV/AIDS education in Ghana. I also took photographs of Billboards

and listened to radio programs on HIV/AIDS education in Ghana. In particular, whilst in Ghana I

listened to an adult education program on fasting. Incidentally my stay coincided with the

Ramadan festival which is a Muslim season of 30 day fast. During the discussion, the

programmer alluded to the fact that Muslims are obligated to fast for 30 days, and from sun

down to sun rise they are to abstain from food and sexual relations with spouses. He said that

likewise, as a means to prevent HIV/AIDS, people should practice abstinence and protect

themselves by using condoms. During the interviews most of the participants referred to this

program as one that had a lasting impact on them.

In analyzing the mass media educational materials collected I looked for relevancy of the

materials. In particular I was interested in finding out if the educational materials appealed to the

people of Savelugu/Nanton in terms of the cultural practices in the area such as multiple sexual

partners. I was also interested in finding out how appropriate the information presented or depicted by the educational materials were to the people. For example, did the educational materials address the cultural beliefs about diseases such as "all die be die"? In addition, I was interested in finding out if the educational materials were written at a level of literacy that primary school students could comprehend. Finally, I was interested in determining if the documents were easily accessible to everyone, because in Ghana, the farther away you are from the urban areas, the more difficult it is to obtain important health information.

Validity and Reliability

Internal validity deals with the question of how research findings match reality (Merriam, 1998). This type of validity asks the question how congruent are my findings with reality? According to Merriam and Simpson (1995) one underlying assumption of the qualitative paradigm is that reality is holistic, multidimensional, ever changing, and is not fixed. For example, my reality of Ghana AIDS education will be different from another person's reality of Ghana's AIDS education. However, there are several strategies that can be adopted to ensure internal validity. Triangulation is a strategy that involves the use of multiple investigators, multiple sources of data, or multiple methods to confirm the emerging findings (Denzin, 1970; Matheson, 1988; Merriam, 1998; Patton, 2002). For example, if the researcher hears about the phenomenon in interviews, sees it taking place in observations, and reads about it in pertinent documents, he or she can be confident that the reality of the situation, as perceived by those in it, is being conveyed as truthfully as possible (Merriam & Simpson, 1995). I used the interview method, documents I collected such as posters, pamphlets, and photographs I took of billboards on HIV/AIDS, and personal field notes as multiple data sources to strengthen the internal validity of the study.

58

Peer or colleague examination is another strategy used in strengthening internal validity in qualitative research. In this case the principal investigator asks peers or colleagues to examine the data and comment on the plausibility of the emerging findings (Merriam, 1998). The assumption here is that those colleagues may be more knowledgeable in the research process than researcher may be. It is also assumed that since the researcher is the main instrument for data collection he/she could miss some important interpretations. I employed peer/colleague examination to add another lens to the interpretation. Dr. Joan Burke and Dr. Mohammed Ibrahim both read through the emerging findings and gave valuable advice. Dr. Mohammed is a native of Ghana and familiar with the area. He was therefore a source for strengthening the internal validity of study.

Another strategy for strengthening the internal validity of a qualitative study is a statement of the researcher's experiences, assumptions, biases or subjectivities at the outset of the study. This enables the reader to better understand how the data might have been interpreted in the manner in which they were. I stated my subjectivities at the beginning of the research process.

External validity entails the extent to which the findings of a study can be applied to other situations. In the past, the issue of generalizability has been problematic for qualitative researchers. Qualitative researchers are asked to view generalizability differently. The most common re-conceptualization is that of user generalizability or reader generalizability. This means that the decision to use the findings rests with the user of the research even though different situations may be involved.

Reliability in the social sciences is problematic because human behaviors are not static, that because what is being studied in education is assumed to be influx, multifaceted, and highly contextual. And because of the emergent design of a qualitative study, it is fanciful to think of reliability within the traditional sense. Several researchers working in the qualitative tradition

59

have re-conceptualized reliability. They see it as the trustworthiness of data to yield the same results over time or whether the "results are consistent with the data collected" Merriam (1998, p. 206).

Researcher Bias

According to Douglass and Moustakas (1984), the first phase in any qualitative study is to identify one's preconceived notions and biases. For example, my personal bias is that everyone can adopt safer sex practices even though this is difficult to achieve in Ghana. I also believe that the Ghana government has not done enough in the past about the problem of HIV/AIDS. However, I believe that these biases did not influence my objectivity in terms of data analysis. By allowing the data to reveal the state of sexual practices in Ghana, I was able to bound these personal assumptions and biases. The rationale for stating personal biases is that by identifying these preconceived notions the researcher endeavors, to gain clarity as he/she proceeds in the research process.

My overriding and personal convictions about HIV/AIDS led me to undertake this research project. I have worked in villages where peoples' understanding of diseases based on local customs and traditions were frightening and at times hard to understand. I have also watched with patience as the availability of information and the format that appealed them suddenly changed their worldviews about diseases. These experiences over the years taught me important lessons that I brought to bear on this study. I believe that when learning is appropriately tailored to people dealing with a health crisis, change in sexual practices may result. However, my interest in HIV/AIDS also has a personal family tragedy side. One of my siblings died suddenly after many years of ailing from an "unknown" disease. I became suspicious because the medical staff failed to diagnose exactly what killed him. Nevertheless, how dare you say to family members that he had died of AIDS? The community perception of the disease at the time was that of retribution for evils done to the gods and a disgrace for one to be associated with the disease. Following this personal tragedy, I decided to help in the fight against HIV/AIDS through education. I believe that everyone needs to better understand the disease and take steps to promote safer sex practices in Ghana. Although this bias is positive, it did not blind me in my understanding of people who failed to identify the disease as a problem in Ghana.

Another bias that I brought to bear on the study is the belief that everyone can make changes in their behavior. I believe that with appropriate information tailored to adults in the community it would not be long before changes in sexual behaviors may occur. As an adult educator, I also believe that learning situations require students to be active participants in their learning processes. All these biases however were countered by an open mind during the analysis.

Chapter Summary

This chapter addressed the methodology employed in this study. The qualitative in-depth interview and document analysis of HIV/AIDS educational materials collected were used. The rational for the choice of the qualitative research paradigm was explained as lending itself to understanding phenomena like sexual practices from the perspectives of participants. I discussed how the interviews were recorded, transcribed, and coded. Further, I explained how themes emerged leading to categories of findings for the study. I discussed my personal biases for undertaking the study. This chapter presented an overview of research methodology used to investigate how Ghanaian adults learned to make changes in their sexual practices in response to HIV/AIDS.

61

CHAPTER FOUR

FINDINGS

Introduction

The purpose of this study was to understand how Ghanaian adults learned to change their

sexual practices in response to the HIV/AIDS crisis. Four central questions that guided this study

were: (1) what changes have Ghanaian adults made in their sexual practices since learning about

HIV/AIDS? (2) how do Ghanaian adults learn formally or informally what they need to know to

make changes in their sexual practices in response to HIV/AIDS? (3) what is the learning

process that leads Ghanaian adults to make changes in their sexual practices in response to

HIV/AIDS? (4) what factors encourage or deter Ghanaian adults from making changes in their

sexual practices in response to the HIV/AIDS crisis?

This chapter presents the findings of the study. The data for this study were obtained

through interviews with ten individuals who had been identified as having made at least one

change in their sexual practices as a preventive measure in response to the HIV/AIDS virus in

the community of (Savelugu/Nanton District) in Ghana. Supplemental analysis entailed

document analysis of HIV/AIDS educational materials used by stakeholders in HIV/AIDS

education in Ghana (posters, billboards, pamphlets).

The sample for this study was obtained through an informant who found an intact group

engaged in HIV/AIDS education. These individuals were identified by the principal informant as

people who had changed their sexual practices.

62

Members of the group carried out HIV/AIDS educational activities through word of mouth, distribution of literature on HIV/AIDS, such as (posters and pamphlets, and condom demonstrations). Another outlet where the group engaged the community in HIV/AIDS education was at cultural and community gatherings like naming ceremonies, marriage ceremonies and traditional festivals. A popular outlet however, remains the weekly market day gathering of members during which new information pertaining to the locality is shared with the public. I was privileged to sit in on one such gathering during the interview process where members engaged the community on condom use, a discussion on the role of population growth in development and HIV/AIDS education. This setting provided the context for the interview of individuals for this study.

Description of the Group

According to the informant the exact date when the group was founded is not certain. However, the group started as a collection of individuals who hailed from Savelugu/Nanton. The mission of the group was to be engaged in community improvement in the Savelugu/Nanton District. The goal of the group is eradication of diseases in the community, especially HIV/AIDS. They usually met weekly to discuss issues of importance to the community. Topics discussed ranged from transportation, child health, politics, sanitation, and agriculture and community improvement. They usually met at the community center and sometimes at the District Assembly meeting room. They occasionally met at homes of people who were willing to provide space for such meetings. The nature of the meetings was informal and allowed participants to freely dialogue on issues happening in the community. They kept minutes of

63

meetings but did not keep a log of attendees. Membership is open and there are no membership

dues or fees. The informant stated that membership fees would prevent a lot of people from

participating in the activities of the group. Membership of the group provides opportunities for

recognition as opinion leaders in the community.

Description of the Participants

Ten members of the group were interviewed in the month of October 2004 in Ghana. The

profile of each participant includes gender, age, highest educational attainment, and marital

status. The profiles are presented in Table 1. Participants consisted of six men and four women.

Their age range was from 26 years to 46 years even though one participant was described as over

sixty years. He could not confirm his age and in line with traditional custom, I did not ask. Eight

members of the group that were interviewed were married whereas two members were single.

The occupation of participants ranged from government workers to non-government workers.

Specifically, some were subsistence farmers, food sellers, butcher, construction worker, health

care worker, a teacher and a social /community development worker. Their educational

attainment was also varied. One participant had a college degree, whereas some participants had

associate degrees. Other participants had basic education.

TABLE 1: Participant Profile

Name	Gender	Age	Job	Education	Status
Abibata	F	33	Trader	High School	M
Adam	M	32	Butcher	Primary	M

Amina	F	X	Food Seller	Primary	M
Grace	F	43	Nurse	Nurse Co.	M
Mariama	F	28	Teacher	Teacher College	S
Mba Ziblim	M	X	Farmer	Primary	M
Mohamed	M	X	Farmer	Primary	M
Salifu	M	34	Foreman	Poly Co.	M
Samad	M	46	Social Worker	College	M
Sumaila	M	26	Clerical	High School	S

The next section gives a brief description of each participant and the change they made as a consequence of learning about HIV/AIDS.

Abibata

Abibata is 33 years old. She is a second wife in a group of three wives. The husband is a small scale farmer but is not a member of the group. She attended a teacher training college for a year and dropped out. She owns a store in the market and sells provisions as a wholesaler to retailers. Abibata came to the group at the invitation of Mariama and Amina. She has been affiliated with the group since 2001. Abibata spoke openly about the use of the female condom

65

as a personal change because of the failure of her husband to use the male condom. She believes

that men in the area are all capable of adopting goods practices to prevent HIV/AIDS but are still

holding on to old cultural believes such as the belief in the supremacy of men over women and

God as the source of diseases in the community. Abibata participates regularly in the activities of

the group during their weekly market day gatherings. Though she wants to see many changes

made by the men she acknowledged that it might take a long time because of her personal

experience with the husband.

Adam

Adam did not give a specific age but insisted he was neither too old nor too young. He is

a butcher. Adam is married to one wife. Adam is very active in the community. He became

aware of HIV/AIDS through a friend who informed him about the disease. Thereafter

membership in the group has been very helpful in providing comfort and support for him to learn

more about the disease and his work environment. Adam mentioned the use of condoms and

remaining faithful to his wife as personal changes he has made since learning about HIV/AIDS.

He also now takes precautions at his workplace to prevent him from contracting HIV/AIDS like

wearing gloves, and being careful with his work tools as a butcher. He has been affiliated with

the group since 1996

Amina

Amina is a small scale restaurant operator (popularly called chop bars in Ghana). She

sells cooked rice and beans (peas) called wache which is a favorite Ghanaian dish. She is a

second wife in a polygamous marriage of four wives. Amina did not volunteer her age and in line

with traditional practices I did not ask for her age. Amina has some high school education but

dropped out due to family pressure to get married and have children. She has three children and

66

is active in the community on matters affecting childhood education and finding self help training for young mothers out of wedlock. In the past she offered employment to young school dropouts called Kayayo.

Amina got involved in the activities of the group after hearing members discuss the menace of HIV/AIDS during a market day gathering. Of particular concern was the practice of extra marital relations of the men in the community. She said that after listening to members of the groups' education on HIV/AIDS and how to prevent it, she realized she was vulnerable because of her marital arrangement. She was particularly worried that the disease had no cure and posed tremendous challenges to healthcare workers.

The attendance at group meetings and especially the weekly market day gathering were very illuminating to her as members helped her to understand the disease and how she could change her sexual practices. She credits the group for helping her adapt to condom use, and to have the strength and strategies to impress upon her husband to remain faithful to his wives. Amina also believes that men and women should be educated to change practices such as having many wives, and having loose sexual relationships, so as to prevent HIV/AIDS.

Though she has been very faithful to her husband she fears the husband has been seeing other women. The use of the female condom has been a "blessing" as she believes it protects her from contracting HIV/AIDS. She has been a member of the group since1997.

Grace

Grace is 43 years old and married with two children. She does not come from Savelugu/Nanton District but has worked there for the past six years as a health educator with the local Health Center. Grace is a Christian and a government health care worker in Savelugu/Nanton and a repository of new information on HIV/AIDS. Her contact with Planned

Parenthood Association of Ghana, the Ghana AIDS Commission and other parties involved in

HIV/AIDS education put her at the forefront in the fight against HIV/AIDS in the area.

According to Samad, Grace has been the main supplier and convener of meetings and

educational materials that members have distributed to others. Everyone refers to her as "madam

condom" because of her advocacy and education on condom use in the community. Grace is a

resource for the group on issues pertaining to women health and condom education. Due to her

work and training in healthcare, she has provided insight and training about HIV/AIDS behavior

change modification strategies to all in the group. As a healthcare worker she has taken special

precautions to prevent contracting HIV/AIDS such as workplace safety.

On a personal note Grace decided to be faithful to her spouse and believes he is faithful

as well. As a principal educator, she has helped not only the women but the men to navigate the

difficulties of remaining faithful, condom use and to avoid loose sexual relations. She is also

very active in the community both officially as a health care worker and as a private resource for

health counseling and education. She has been a member of the group his 1998.

Mariama

Mariama is 28 years old female primary school teacher from a nearby community but

resides in Savelugu/Nanton District. Mariama volunteered her age. She graduated from a teacher

training college and is currently pursuing a long distance graduate education program. She is not

married but is currently in a relationship and hopes to marry soon. She came to the group through

a mutual friend of Samad. Mariama believes that a lot of work still needs to be done to

encourage women to adopt changes in their personal practices to prevent HIV/AIDS. According

to her, she was surprised by the lack of concern many parents continue to show in regards to the

education of their children. Mariama believes that women in the community need to assert

68

themselves on matters that affect their reproductive health, such as the number of children they should have, premarital HIV/AIDS testing and counseling and the practice of polygamy (having more than one wife and additional relationships outside of marriage).

Of particular concern to Mariama is the culture of loose sexual practices and multiple sexual partners. Accordingly she has adopted abstinence and faithfulness as personal changes in her life to prevent HIV. She has also educated a lot of friends on the need to avoid multiple sexual partners and to adapt practices such as being faithful to one sexual partner as a means of HIV/AIDS prevention. She has been an active member of the group and a resource for other women since 1998.

Mba Ziblim

Mba Ziblim is a member of the traditional ruling family and a community elder. He did not volunteer his age, and in line with custom I did not ask for his age. But Mohammed, a distance nephew of Mba Ziblim, believes he is in his 60s. Mba Ziblim is a farmer and a repository of customs and traditions of the community. He cultivates corn, guinea corn, and millet and raises cattle, goats, and sheep. He is married and has six wives. Mba Ziblim has some form of primary education but did not attend high school because in his younger day's school attendance was seen as a waste of time. He was therefore groomed for his present position as a sub-chief (junior chief) by learning from the elders of the palace and his father. Currently he manages skin lands (land vested in traditional authority in Northern Ghana) and oversees the operations of the market. He has been affiliated with the group since 1997.

As a member of the ruling family, Mba Ziblim is desirous of bringing development to the area by helping in job creation and civic mobilization. He is well respected and is seen as a bridge between old customs and traditions of the village and the adoption of new ones. He narrated his adaptation of condom use as one of the most difficult decisions he has made as an

adult in response to HIV/AIDS in the community. Though an ardent supporter of the group in its

educational activities, he still maintains that cultural norms such as the role of women, and some

forms of polygamy should still be permitted in the community because the society has survived

on these customs and traditions for a long time.

Mohammed

Mohammed is married to two wives and has eight children. He has some primary

education but due to lack of interest in school he did not go to high school. He is small scale

farmer during the farming season (April to September) and a butcher (he owns and operates a

meat shop in the market). He cultivates corn, rice, and yam, and also raises goats, sheep and

cows. He did not volunteer his age and joked that his parents never told him when he was born.

Mohammed volunteers at the local mosque and helps in spreading the message of abstinence,

faithfulness, and condom use to prevent HIV/AIDS in the community. He has internalized the

message of the group by being faithful to his wives.

However, Mohammed laments that he did not come into contact with the group early

enough to know the advantages of monogamy and faithfulness. He also believes that in general

the culture in which men are the head of the household and makes all the decisions that affect

women should change. In addition, he believes that his membership of the group has provided

him with opportunities for learning about himself and his community. Mohammed believes that

this knowledge about the disease and his environment has improved his business, personal

growth and development. He has been a member of the group since 1999. Accordingly, he

personally invited other butchers to join the group to enable them to begin to understand the

nature of HIV/AIDS and to appreciate preventive education on HIV/AIDS.

Salifu

Salifu is a 34 year old male from Savelugu/Nanton. Salifu is a graduate of the regional

polytechnic in Tamale, and majored in building technology. Salifu volunteered his age. Salifu

works for the District of Savelugu/Nanton and also as a foreman for a building contractor. He is

also a small scale farmer and cultivates corn. He is married and has three children. He first came

into contact with the activities of the group through a friend. He believes that Savelugu/Nanton

District has been wrongly labeled a town of loose sexual activities to some extent, as it is on the

main Ghana-Burkina-Faso thoroughfare.

Salifu wants to see changes in the way members of the community think about

HIV/AIDS. His passion and enthusiasm for community improvement has taken him to villages,

and towns. He says he developed a special knack for teaching the younger generation about

HIV/AIDS because they are the future of the community. His educational efforts also attack

loose sexual practices such as the practice of prostitution in the area.

Salifu credits his friends and group members for being a resource for his learning and

continued strength in remaining HIV free. He has practiced the use of condoms and until his

marriage practiced abstinence. In line with group learning Salifu has remained loyal and faithful

to his wife and children in marriage. He also believes that the use of condoms should be widely

promoted to curtail other sexually transmitted diseases like gonorrhea and syphilis. Salifu has

been associated with the activities of the group since 2000.

Samad

Samad is a 46 year old native of Savelugu/Nanton District. He is college educated and

works in community/social development. He is also a small scale farmer. Samad volunteered his

age. He is a non elected member of the Savelugu/Nanton District Assembly. Samad is about five

71

feet six inches tall and fair in color. Samad is married to one wife and has two sons.

Samad is active in the community on issues of education health and economic improvement. He is the principal organizer of the group and serves as the avant-garde (innovator) and repository of knowledge on HIV/AIDS. The idea of bringing together friends and family to dialogue on matters affecting the community was nothing new to him. As a child he said, "he always went with my father to gatherings during which they talk about bringing electricity to our village." During his college years he said he realized that many people came to him for information on many matters such as education and community improvement. The idea of a group comprising of men and women to learn was borne out of his curiosity and desire to share knowledge with those less fortunate to go to college. As the facilitator of the group his main concern now is the prevention and eradication of all diseases in the area especially malaria and HIV/AIDS and to encourage nongovernmental organizations to bring development to the area. Samad is compassionate about his role and his desire to bring improvement to the community.

Samad has teamed up with the Ghana AIDS Commission to provide condoms free of charge to members of the community. He has a good working relationship with the local Health Center to conduct HIV/AIDS testing for all in the community. Though not sure of the exact date of formation of the group, nevertheless, Samad believes the group has been around since 1995. According to Samad he learned about HIV/AIDS during his college days in Accra in 1993 through friends, professors, and healthcare workers on campus. As a consequence of learning about HIV/AIDS he decided to practice abstinence prior to marriage. Now in marriage he remains faithful to his wife. Another change Samad made was the adoption of condom use.

In his marriage Samad believes that the most important change he has made is the

72

adaptation of condom use. This is significant because of traditional beliefs about condoms being

designed to make men impotent in Africa. Culturally, Samad believes that old customs and

traditions about women being responsible for diseases in the community need to be changed. He

also believes that as a native of the community people will listen to him better than strangers

who come to educate people about HIV/AIDS in the community. He sees his involvement as a

way of giving back to his community.

Sumaila

Sumaila is twenty-six years old. He volunteered to tell me his age. He is single but is

currently dating only one woman. Sumaila is a high school graduate and a clerical staff of the

Savelugu/Nanton District Administration. He is very active in civic affairs of the community in

his capacity as a native of the area and as a civil servant. He has been a member of the group

since 2000. Sumaila believes that the younger generation needs to take up the challenge of

HIV/AIDS education because they are those yet to marry and in order to get a good wife that

wife must be tested for HIV/AIDS. Sumaila believes that his loyalty and faithfulness to his

girlfriend is reinforced by the group through their weekly meetings. He acknowledged that he

practiced abstinence for a long time until he met his fiancée and prays that the youth will do the

same.

Changes Made in Sexual Practices

An analysis of the participants' discussion indicates that they made three different types

of changes in sexual practices. These were 1) Adhering to sexual abstinence until marriage, 2)

Limiting the number of sexual partners, and 3) Adopting the use of condoms.

Adhering to Sexual Abstinence until Marriage

Abstinence is the appreciation and practice of sexual purity until marriage. It may also be described as avoiding premarital sex. Whereas some abstinence programs encourage abstinence only, some programs promote abstinence with other forms of HIV prevention such as condom use. When asked what behaviors they had adopted since learning about HIV/AIDS, Salifu related the following: "I practiced abstinence until I got married. I encourage my friends who are not yet married to practice abstinence."

Samad narrated that he practiced abstinence until he got married and also insisted that this was in consonance with information he learned about practicing abstinence as a measure to prevent HIV/AIDS. Samad indicated that abstinence was one area where his Islamic faith also supported literature on HIV/AIDS. In addition, as part of his educational outreach to members of the group and the community, he encourages the principles of abstinence. This is an excerpt from our conversation on the subject:

It is abstinence that I practiced until marriage. We members of the group encourage the

people to abstain particularly the youth and young adults from sex and to marry,

otherwise if you are going to have sex use condoms. The demand for condoms now is

very high and this tells us that our education is very effective in the community.

Grace said she welcomed the practice of abstinence because she learned it as a youth to prevent sexually transmitted diseases such as syphilis, and now learning that HIV/AIDS is sexually transmitted, she become even more resolved in that decision to abstain. Grace said, "Until I got married I practiced abstinence." Commenting on the practice of sexual abstinence in her work with the group and the community she said, the practice of abstinence was beginning to be understood by not only members of the group but by majority of the population. This was

74

because the teachings about abstinence are being complimented by religious leaders in the community. Grace recalled how a member of the group, Mohammed, came to her for an explanation on the practice of abstinence. During their discussion Mohammed explained that he married his first wife as a virgin so he believed he abstained prior to their marriage and they all laughed about it.

Limiting Sexual Partners

Another change made by participants who were married or who engaged in sexual activities prior to marriage was a reduction in the number of sexual partners they had. This took various forms such as the faithfulness before marriage, faithfulness in monogamous marriage, and faithfulness in polygamous marriage. This change in sexual practice is significant because as a society influenced by the teachings of Islam, the practice of having multiple sexual partners is acceptable. The cultural norms of the ethnic society also support the practice of polygamy and having many children. Thus as a consequence of this latitude, extra marital affairs, and multiple sexual activities are common. This section, therefore, examines the practice of reducing the number of sexual partners as a response to HIV/AIDS in the community. Within this category are faithfulness to a partner before marriage, monogamous marriage and faithfulness, and polygamous marriage and faithfulness to spouses.

Faithfulness before marriage. Participants also reported that after learning about the dangers of HIV/AIDS, they decided to practice faithfulness in their relationships before marriage. According to Mariama who is single, whereas the use of condoms is desirable for preventing HIV/AIDS, in her opinion reducing the number of sexual partners and being faithful to your partner is by far more important in preventing HIV/AIDS in the community. She stated:

I hate men who have extra marital affairs. And I do not like women who cheat on their

75

husbands. I believe multiple sexual partners are not good. I have one sexual partner

because of the education I received from Grace about the dangers involved in contracting

HIV/AIDS.

To Sumaila who is single, knowing about the dangers of HIV/AIDS have made him to be

sincere with his girlfriend and expects that she will reciprocate by being faithful before their

marriage.

This was what he said:

I have resolved to remain faithful to my girlfriend in line with what my knowledge about

HIV/AIDS is. I know that being faithful is one way of preventing HIV/AIDS. I know I

am faithful and I hope she is also faithful.

Sumaila, who is unmarried, being faithful in his relationship with a one woman, is a sure

way of protection against HIV/AIDS. He remarked that some people know the disease is real

inside their heart but on the outside they say the disease is not real to enable them to continue

doing bad things to women. He said:

For me, since learning about the disease I don't go after women anymore. I am not yet

married but I have one girlfriend and I am faithful to her. Really we know that amorous

sexual relationships are not good as they can lead to HIV/AIDS.

Faithfulness in monogamous marriage. Another avenue where changes in sexual

practice were expressed was in being faithful in a monogamous relationship. By adhering to the

tenets of their marriage and avoiding extra-marital affairs, participants were able to overcome

their cultural and religious practices that supported extra-marital relations whether in marriage or

not. This section discusses faithfulness in monogamous relationships as a measure adopted by

participants to prevent HIV/AIDS.

Salifu, a married participant also said that he now believes in having one sexual partner as a way of preventing HIV/AIDS because of the discussions they have had about the dangers of multiple sexual partners as high risks behavior for contracting the new disease. He stated, "I do not court women anymore even though I used to as it was a good thing to do before I got married."

Grace, a married healthcare worker said, "One important change I have made is to be faithful to my husband." Continuing, she said that in her encounter with other women who come to the health center, "they report that they have also been faithful to their spouses and believe that most Ghanaians have remained faithful to their partners in marriage as a result of learning about HIV/AIDS."

Samad, a participant with one wife explained that "I am married to one wife and I am faithful. I wonder why people are not faithful to their partners." One other change that was recurrent was the new found faithfulness to spouses in polygamous marriages. The next section therefore takes a brief look at what participants said about faithfulness as a behavior learned to prevent HIV/AIDS in their polygamous marriages in the community.

Faithfulness in a polygamous marriage. Faithfulness here is being true to marriage partners. This is in contrast to the accepted cultural practice where the male is married to many women and can have relations with other women outside of the marriage. A recurring theme during the interviews was reference to the practice of faithfulness. Even though some participants are married to more than one wife they extolled the virtues of faithfulness. They believe that they have made their mistakes by marrying more than one wife. However, by sticking to these wives only, they are being faithful. Commenting on being faithful, Mba Ziblim a traditional elder of the community gave this perspective on faithfulness when he said:

I have many wives, and I tell them that I will not bring another woman into the family. I

tell them that I am faithful to all of them and expect them to do the same. It will be a

disgrace to me when I hear that one of my wives is in a relationship with another man.

Mohammed, a polygamist with two wives said that the group has been helpful in teaching him

about reducing the number of sexual partners as a way of preventing and contracting HIV/AIDS.

He said that through group discussions he has adopted the practice of sticking with his spouses

and not having extra-marital affairs outside his marriage.

Mohammed said:

I reason that I know the HIV status of my wife but I do not know that of other women

because I cannot convince them to take the HIV test. I also know that the same girlfriend

is probably in a relationship with another man that I don't know. So the best prevention I

can provide myself is to avoid extra-marital relationship.

Furthermore, Mohammed narrated that through the educational activities of the group he

has not only remained faithful but has not taken an additional wife. He said, "Everybody thinks I

am a fool because I have a good business and money but only two wives." According to

Mohammed this decision was difficult because wealth and marriage in the community are seen

as signs of success.

To Amina, who is a second wife in a polygamous relationship, women in the area should

be blamed for helping the men have extra marital affairs. According to her, she has now learned

to say no to men when they make proposals to her even though they know she is married and

faithful to the husband. Amina wished she had been given this education on the dangers of

multiple partners and the need for being faithful in a polygamous marriage as an avenue for

contracting HIV/AIDS much earlier. She lamented that earlier in her youth she played along with

78

other women who had multiple boyfriends. She stated:

> In a way it is the fault of women because they know that this man is already married and
>
> yet when he approaches you saying I am interested in you the women don't say no. Well
>
> I say no to encourage my friends who have not yet joined our group to reduce the number
>
> of boyfriends they have and my male friends to reduce the number of girlfriends they
>
> have. Not having any sexual relationships with men who are already married will help
>
> prevent HIV/AIDS.

Adopting the Use of Condoms

A third change in sexual practice was to adopt the use of condoms when engaging in sexual activities. This was true for both male and female participants. Mariama recounted her decision to adopt the practice of condom use. She said: "The idea of using condoms and not having many boyfriends was a practice I learned from this group because of the education I got from members."

Mba Ziblim, also recounted his adoption of condom use and stated, "It is difficult to tell you the changes I have made, but let me say it is condom use. I have a lot of them and I use them." Amina in her comment on the use of condoms said:

> It is very important that I use condoms to protect myself because my husband has two
>
> other wives and I don't know where everyone (woman) goes apart from our home. I don't
>
> even know where my husband goes every time. I know my condom is my best safeguard.

Abibata, a married woman in a polygamous relationship recounted that because the culture and traditions of the community will not permit her to ask her husband to use condom, she made the decision to use the female condom. This is what she said in our conversation on the subject, "I use condoms since you are not the only wife of your husband. I use personal

79

protection like the female condoms, because culturally the men do not want you to tell them to use the male condom."

In a related remark, Mba Ziblim, an elder of the community also said, apart from adopting the use of condoms himself he is also encouraging his people to use them. This was what he said: "I am encouraging my subjects to reduce sexual activities and to use condoms to prevent HIV/AIDS as I have already done."

Samad said that, "I use condoms always and every organization involved in HIV/AIDS education in the area (Ghana AIDS Commission, World Vision and National AIDS Control Program) supports the use of condoms."

Three changes were made by participants in their sexual practices in response to HIV/AIDS education in Savelugu/Nanton. These were adhering to abstinence until marriage, limiting the number of sexual partners, and the adoption of condom use. Two sub-categories were also discussed within the category of limiting the number of sexual partners. In both monogamous and polygamous relationships, participants also practiced faithfulness in response to curbing the spread of HIV/AIDS as a result of group activities and education.

The Role of Learning in Changing Sexual Practices

The section explains how participants learned to make changes in their sexual practices. The predominant form of learning that participants used to learn about HIV/AIDS and also to make changes in their sexual practices was informal learning. In this section, the researcher examined first how participants initially became aware of the new disease and second what they did after their initial encounter. For example, the researcher identified and recorded the individual learning they did, and the group activities they engaged in that led them to make changes in the sexual practices. The process of learning is presented in table 2.

80

Table 2: The Process of Learning

Becoming Aware of HIV/AIDS

    From people

    Mass media

Catalyst for Further Learning

    Fear of death

    Social stigma of AIDS in the community

Learning about HIV/AIDS

    Consulted with other individuals

    Group learning activities

Other Factors That Influenced Change Adoption

    Cultural factors

    Religion

Table 2 describes how participants learned to make changes in their sexual practices in response to HIV/AIDS in Savelugu/Nanton District of Ghana. The learning process began with participants becoming aware of the disease. Information about the disease came from a friend or a mass media source. Two factors motivated participants to learn about the disease. These were the fear of death, and the social stigma of the disease in the community. These two factors were the catalysts that encouraged further learning. The learning occurred in an informal manner and involved consulting with individuals and engaging in group activities. The changed sexual practices that participants adopted were adhering to abstinence prior to marriage, limiting the number of sexual partners and adoption of condom use. Culture and religion were other factors that influenced change adoption in response to HIV/AIDS in Savelugu/Nanton District of Ghana.

Becoming Aware of HIV/AIDS

Two sources were identified in the discussion on how participants become aware of the new disease. First, participants learned about HIV/AIDS by being informed by a friend, or a relative. The second way was through the mass media, such as posters, billboards, the radio or information they read from pamphlets about HIV/AIDS.

From other people. Most participants said that they heard about HIV/AIDS from friends. This was how Salifu learned about HIV/AIDS:

I went to Kumasi (Ghana's second largest city) for a job interview and lodged with a friend and during conversation he asked me if I knew about the new disease called HIV/AIDS. I said "no" so he brought me some booklets on HIV/AIDS and asked me to read them. After reading them I knew HIV/AIDS was a very harmful disease.

Grace a healthcare worker related that she became aware of HIV/AIDS from a medical doctor at the health center. Thereafter, the Ministry of Health organized an in- service education and training in Accra for healthcare workers on HIV/AIDS which she attended. Grace recalled, "I learned about HIV/AIDS, from a medical doctor and through in service education in Accra about 1984."

Mba Ziblim said he heard about the disease from the District Administrator (Mayor). He recalled, "The District Administrator informed me about the new disease and asked that I should inform my people, so I invited him to one of our community gatherings and he explained the whole matter to us."

82

Samad said he heard about the disease in his college days from his professors and friends. Sumaila also heard about HIV/AIDS from friends in the community. Amina another participant also learned about HIV/AIDS from friends. A predominant form through which participants learned about HIV/AIDS initially was from people who gave them information about the disease. The next section examines mass media sources for learning about HIV/AIDS in Savelugu/Nanton District of Ghana.

Mass media. Another medium through which information about HIV/AIDS was received was from pamphlets, magazines, radio, television, billboards and posters. These posters and billboards were placed at schools, on major roads, at the healthcare centers, and at market centers to attract people by the Ghana National Commission on AIDS, and the Ghana AIDS Control Program.

Mass media is the term used to denote that section of the media specifically conceived and designed to reach a very large audience, at least the whole population or nation. It was coined in the early 1920s with the advent of nationwide radio networks and mass circulation newspapers and magazines. The mass media audience has been viewed by some commentators as forming a mass society with special characteristics, notably atomization or lack of connections, which render it especially susceptible to the influence of modern mass media technique such as advertising and propaganda.

As a strategy of HIV/AIDS education, the mass media have been used extensively to distribute HIV/AIDS education materials in Ghana. With reference to mass media channels of learning about HIV/AIDS, Mariama also recalled learning about HIV/AIDS on the radio in Togo a neighboring country to Ghana. She stated:

I went to Togo to visit family members and whilst listening to the radio a cousin drew

my attention to the new disease. She said the disease attacks your immune system

making it difficult for you to fight any disease. This was scary to me so I decided to

look for more information about the disease.

Mohammed related how he learned about HIV for the first time. "I heard about

HIV/AIDS from a friend who showed me some pamphlets on the disease. Later I learned that my

wife also found out about the disease from the big billboard near the market square."

Sumaila remarked,

It's been a while since I started hearing about HIV/AIDS. First, I heard it from a friend

and later on the radio. Look around you; you will see it on posters, billboards at the

market square; simply everywhere an HIV/AIDS picture is starring at you.

During the discussion Abibata said:

I heard about HIV/AIDS on the radio and I have since been listening to the "Radio

Doctor" [a weekly magazine program about health education in Ghana]. Every week on

the program there is a discussion about HIV/AIDS and how to prevent HIV/AIDS. I

wonder why some people still claim they have not heard about this disease.

Using the criteria of document analysis, I analyzed the mass media and derived these

findings. First, with respect to the posters, they did not adequately depict a typical Ghanaian

HIV/AIDS patient. In particular in the North the dress code is different from the Southern parts

of the country but this was not reflected in the posters. What is interesting was that all the posters

that depicted Ghanaians actually depicted good looking middle class Ghanaians and not the

population hardest hit by HIV/AIDS. Second, no posters were published in the local language.

All posters were in English the official language of Ghana. Sadly, however, not all Ghanaians can read and write in English. The impact of the posters might have been more effective if they had been published in the local languages and depicted people from the north. It would have been beneficial if some of the local languages had been used in the design of the posters to give it a more local and authentic flavor.

Third, the billboards also depicted HIV/AIDS patients and carried various messages on prevention education. The billboard messages strikingly portrayed fear of death associated with HIV/AIDS. Images depicted human skeletal remains showing the consequences of the disease. The fear associated with these messages appears to have attracted the attention of people in the research area about the need to adopt measures to prevent HIV/AIDS.

The media appear to have concentrated on the fatal consequences of the disease and this may have been responsible for gaining people attention to the disease. Again, participants said they were informed about the disease through the medium of these billboards. The billboards provided participants information that made them curious to learn about the new disease.

Information about HIV/AIDS from the radio also emphasized the fatal consequences of HIV/AIDS. Messages from radio programs gave grave statistics about HIV/AIDS and encouraged people to practice safer sex by adopting the use of condoms. Though these mass media educational materials did not depict the social and cultural traditions of the research area such as dress codes and the language, yet participants nevertheless claimed to have been informed by these mass media channels of health information dissemination.

Catalyst for Further Learning

From this initial learning, participants admitted that the information made them feel the need for change. There were two catalysts that encouraged the participants to learn more about HIV/AIDS. These were the fear of death, and the social stigma of the disease.

Fear of death. Mariama a participant and single, said that the fear of death

contributed to her decision to seek more information about HIV/AIDS. She said:

When I first heard about HIV/AIDS and the fact that when you contract it there is no cure

but suffering and death, I was so worried that I decided to learn more about it. I discussed

my fears with my friends who asked that I contact Grace because she knew a lot about

the new disease. They also suggested I could take the HIV/AIDS test at her clinic. But

when I met Grace she invited me for a discussion on how women could protect

themselves and their families from the disease. She showed me a lot of pamphlets and

booklets on HIV/AIDS prevention education. After reading these materials she asked me

to keep them and share them with other friends who wanted to learn more about the new

disease. We have been friends since and she also introduced me to Samad's group and I

am now a member. I attend the discussions whenever I can as any new information on the

disease is shared with members. Now I also educate a lot of people about HIV/AIDS in

other villages especially the Kayayo (porters who practice prostitution) on how to adopt

safeguards against HIV/AIDS. I believe I have gained a lot by being associated with this

group because I can talk freely about HIV/AIDS prevention with other women who are

my friends. As a teacher my students ask a lot of questions about HIV/AIDS and being

associated with the activities of the group and Grace has provided answers to most of the

questions students ask me.

In another discussion on the subject of fear of the disease as an impetus for seeking

further knowledge, Sumaila, a participant narrated that he was confused and emotional when he

realized that unlike other diseases, HIV/AIDS led to death. He said:

Knowing that once you had it you were going to die was too hard for me to understand. I wondered aloud what I could do to avoid getting this life sentence. Eventually I was led

to the health center where I enquired about things to do to avoid this disease. The

education I got put me in contact with Azindow and Samad and later study discussions by

members of the group.

Furthermore, Sumaila said, "I fear that if people in our community don't get serious about

believing that HIV/AIDS is real we will all die."

The social stigma of HIV/AIDS. During discussions on the social stigma of HIV/AIDS in

the community, participants remarked that recently a woman was beaten to death because of the

fear that she had contracted HIV/AIDS in the community. According to Samad, the social

stigma of the disease is strong, so as a group they are educating not only members but the

community to show compassion to people living with the disease.

Samad said:

> In our community nobody wants to be associated with the disease. This is why
>
> nobody owns up to say they have a family member with the disease. For me I
>
> don't want my family to become outcasts in the society because of HIV/AIDS so I
>
> decided to educate myself about the disease and others in the community.

In our discussions on stigma of HIV/AIDS, another participant, Grace remarked that

when you ask people if they know anybody with the disease they will tell you no, whereas she

knows there are people with the disease in the community. She cannot divulge the names of

people who have tested positive to HIV because of confidentiality.

Grace said:

> In my work I try to adopt all safeguards to avoid contracting the disease because if people
>
> know I have the disease they will not come to the health center for anything. This stigma

reminds me always to remain free of the disease in the community.

Another participant Mohammed also said, "Nobody owns up to say I am HIV-positive. It is too dangerous to do that in our community. The best thing to do is to understand the disease by learning more about it."

In her contribution on the social stigma of the disease as a catalyst for seeking further knowledge about HIV/AIDS, Amina, a participant said:

People will not like to marry from your family. You cannot be invited to any community gathering as people may try to kill you. I don't want any of these for my family so I decided to educate myself on the new disease.

Learning About HIV/AIDS

To continue their education about HIV/AIDS and to adopt preventive measures to remain free of HIV/AIDS, participants engaged in two types of informal learning activities. The first learning activity was that participants consulted with other people about HIV/AIDS. The second learning activity was that they participated in group activities about HIV/AIDS education. The catalysts for this decision were the fear of death, and the social stigma of HIV/AIDS in the community.

Consulted with other individuals. Mohammed, a participant said that the fear of HIV/AIDS motivated him to begin to understand the disease better by seeking knowledge and information from friends, healthcare workers, and others in the community. This search led him to Samad and eventually the group. Mohammed then began sharing learning activities with group members through weekly discussions. This included attendance at market day gatherings where information on the disease, condom use, and literature about HIV/AIDS was distributed to members and the community. Mohammed stated that anytime there is something new that he

88

does not understand he informs Grace about it and at their next meeting it is brought up for discussion. Mohammed stated:

I initially had difficulty understanding why the disease could not be cured. So I approached Grace and Samad. At the group meeting we discussed that the disease destroyed ones ability to fight other diseases and as a virus doctors have not yet developed any vaccines to make people immune to it. This was how I began to understand the nature of the disease.

The understanding that HIV/AIDS had no cure was a motivating factor for participants' decision to seek knowledge that helped them to adopt safeguards to protect themselves and their families.

Mariama another participant also stated:

When I first heard about HIV/AIDS and the knowledge that when you contract it there is no cure but suffering, I was very worried so I decided to learn more about it. I discussed my fears with my friends who asked that I contact Grace because she knew a lot about the new disease. They also suggested I could take the HIV/AIDS test at her clinic. But when I met Grace she invited me for a discussion on how women could protect themselves and their families. She showed me a lot of pamphlets and booklets on HIV/AIDS prevention education. After reading these materials she asked me to keep them and to share them with other friends who wanted to learn more about the new disease. We have been friends since and she also introduced me to Samad's group and I am now a member. I attend the discussions whenever I can as any new information on the disease is shared with members. Now I also educate a lot of people about HIV/AIDS in other villages especially the Kayayo Girls (porters who practice prostitution) on how to

89

protect them. I believe that I have gained a lot by being a member of the group because I

can talk freely about HIV/AIDS prevention with men and women who are not my

friends. As a teacher my students ask a lot of questions about HIV/AIDS and membership

of the group has provided answers to some of the questions they ask me.

In her contribution on the topic Amina said this about her individual learning activities:

My friend said the disease was a very bad disease and that when you get it there is no

cure. It also leads to lots of suffering for people who have the disease. This prompted me

to begin to ask questions about the new disease. I approached my friend Abibata who

asked me to attend a market day gathering on the disease. At the gathering I saw a

demonstration of the various ways you can contract the disease and also the ways you can

protect yourself. The group also distributed free condoms and pamphlets on the new

disease. This was how I got involved in the activities of the group just to learn more

about the new disease.

In addition, another participant Salifu also narrated how he came to the group and began

his journey about learning to make changes in his sexual practices:

My friend said HIV/AIDS has no cure when you contract it you cant be cured. The fear

and disgrace to family members when you die of AIDS was so difficult for me so I

decided to learn more about it and to change my sexual practices. This motivated me to

begin to find out more about the disease. At my workplace a friend told me about free

condoms from the health center, so we decided to go there for some. Unfortunately, we

were rather given education on the new disease by Grace who referred us to Samad. This

was how we joined the group and have been members since. What we do is just learn

about the disease, educate others about the disease and discuss matters affecting our community. I take pride in doing these things because a lot of family members listen when I advise them on the dangers of the disease.

Mohammed said:

After learning about the disease I approached my friend Adam who disclosed that we could get more information on the new disease from the health center. When we went to the health center, we met a number of officials who directed us to see the officer in charge of condom distribution. He welcomed us and wanted to know why we were there. We told him of our desire to learn about the new disease. This officer showed us a video on HIV/AIDS with a group of people. After watching the video it was time to ask questions. I asked if I could come back for more explanation and he said yes. Later Azindow, a worker at the health center referred us to Grace who asked us to contact Samad for further explanation. Samad then invited us to attend a discussion on the subject with some friends that we knew in the evening. This was how we joined the group. Since then through group discussions, information from members, and at times lectures we have come to understand the nature of HIV/AIDS, and what we have to do to prevent contracting the disease.

The next section examines learning in group activities. This includes what members did at naming ceremonies, group meetings, and market day gatherings aimed at reinforcing learned behaviors in support of remaining free of HIV/AIDS.

Involvement with an HIV/AIDS education group. Learning also occurred during organized group activities in an informal way. During the discussions participants said that they were very supportive of each other and helped inform each other any new material to learn on the new disease. Participants stated that the basic purpose for coming together was to learn to

91

adopt a healthy life style to prevent HIV/AIDS in the community. The principal reason for joining the group was to learn about preventing HIV/AIDS as a first step towards leading a healthy lifestyle in the community.

They therefore strived to achieve this goal by adopting life-changing practices. For example pregnancies by members of the group provided opportunities for members to educate each other and the community about HIV/AIDS. For example, Amina said:

When I was pregnant and went to the healthcare center, the maternity nurse asked if I will be willing to take the test for HIV/AIDS. In response I said "yes." Later I met Abibata who decided that we should discuss it with members of the group. I remember that at our next meeting we talked about pregnancy, the HIV/AIDS test, good delivery practices, remaining free of blood contamination, and other issues.

Abibata in her contribution on the subject also said:

During the naming ceremony of my last baby, we invited all members of the community especially young people who are yet to marry. At the ceremony, the Mallam (Muslim teacher/Preacher) talked about the new disease and the need to adopt safeguards to prevent HIV/AIDS so that all members of the community will have healthy babies like me.

Continuing, Abibata said that this sermon was what members of the group used to reach out to others in the community who came to celebrate at the naming ceremony. "We talked to people especially those yet to marry about the dangers of HIV/AIDS and the need to adopt safer sex practices."

Another participant, Samad said that "the group actually welcomed such occasions to help not only members learn about the disease but also to teach people about the disease."

92

Another group activity that members used to learn was that they occasionally invited a speaker to talk to members about HIV/AIDS and Education in the community. According to Sumaila these talks have been very informative because the resource persons that have been invited have given very good education about the disease. Grace reported that they had invited the District Medical Officer to talk about HIV/AIDS in Northern Ghana with particular focus on Savelugu/Nanton.

Grace said "the doctor gave a talk on how the virus was now prevalent in the area and wondered why." Amina, said, she found the lectures informative because it afforded her the opportunity to ask questions about the female condom and other family planning methods. Mba Ziblim, said the doctor explained more about the disease and condom use than he had done previously: "I like the one on one approach because the topic involved sexual practices and I could not ask the same questions in public as I do in the group." Another resource person was the Director of Planned Parenthood Association of Ghana who talked about family planning, contraceptives, and condom use. Mohammed also said that at other times they have discussed politics of the area and how to improve the local schools in the District. He explained "At our meetings we talk about our area and what is going on in the community. We want people here to send their children to school and the government needs to build more schools."

In learning about HIV/AIDS, the initial process began with information from a friend, or from a mass media source such as radio, billboards or pamphlets. After this initial encounter participants were motivated to learn about the new disease because of fear of death and the social stigma of the disease. Subsequent learning led participants to the activities of the group. Further learning opportunities were provided through the support group activities such as naming ceremonies, lectures, weekly discussions, and weekly market day gatherings. Group membership

93

also provided support for further learning. The information and education group members shared

was instrumental in their adaptations of changed practices that helped them to remain free of

HIV in the community. Participants also shared their perspectives on two factors that at times

contributed to learning about HIV/AIDS, but at other times challenged learning about

HIV/AIDS.

Factors that Encouraged or Deterred Change in Sexual Practices

In addition to the goal of understanding how Ghanaian adults learned to make changes in

their sexual practices, I also looked for factors that appeared to influence their learning either in

supportive way or as a deterrent. Understanding these factors may help us structure or reevaluate

our current educational approaches about HIV/AIDS education. Two factors emerged in the

discussions about obstacles to learning and encouragement to learning. What is interesting about

these factors is that they were perceived by participants as both supportive and deterrent to

change in sexual practices. For example, cultural practices such as polygamy and multiple

sexual relationships were a deterrent to change and at the same time polygamy and multiple

sexual relationships encouraged participants to change their sexual practices.

The influence of culture. Cultural practices in the community deterred change in sexual

practices. Of these cultural practices, polygamy, lactation period [the practice of leaving a

marital home until a baby is weaned], gender [ascribed role of women as subservient to men in

the community] the belief that death is destined, and the will of God regardless of it's form and

nature, all negate the adoption of preventive measures to combat the spread of HIV/AIDS. On

the one hand during the discussions, participants stated that it was also because of these same

cultural factors that they had decided to make changes in their sexual practices to prevent

HIV/AIDS.

94

On the cultural practices that make it difficult for husbands in the community to remain faithful during the period of lactation, Abibata captured these frustrations in this narration after persistently trying to make the husband change his ways:

I will tell you a story about our practice of not visiting your husband at night when you have a baby (lactation period). You see I can have any relationship with him even with my baby, but they don't like it because they just want the freedom to see somebody else. The sad part is that at night when I try to visit his bedroom he gives excuses that he is tired due to work whilst in actual fact he has had his satisfaction for the day.

For Abibata, the period of lactation provided the opportunity for learning more about HIV/AIDS, group work and community outreach that eventually encouraged her to change her sexual practices. She said, "I have failed to convince him to change his ways but I can protect myself with the female condom."

According to Mba Ziblim, "It is only a weak Dagomba [member of ethnic group] who marries only one wife." This is because the number of wives a man can take and have determines your wealth and stature in the community. Since no member of the society wants to be seen as weak people are encouraged to marry more than one. This practice is a major deterrent to change in sexual practices in the community.

Another cultural belief that is an obstacle to change is the belief that "all die be die." This was what Salifu said, "I know there is HIV/AIDS because the Government says there is HIV/AIDS. I also believe that all die be die so whatever death God gives me is alright." On the contrary, Mariama believes that the principle of all die be die encouraged change in her sexual practices. She said, I know all (die be die) but I don't want to die before my time is due by behaving carelessly and getting HIV/AIDS."

95

Mba Ziblim an elder of the community said, "Culture is culture. We have been doing these things for years and our community has survived on these practices so why change them now?" "On the contrary it is precisely the understanding that all is not well with current sexual practices such as multiple partners, and extra-marital affairs that encouraged Salifu to adopt changes in his sexual practices. Salifu said "I now know that HIV/AIDS is transmitted sexually so limiting the number of partners is a good safeguard against contracting the HIV/AIDS." Another participant Sumaila also said:

> I will say it is the culture that deters people from making changes in their sexual
> practices. People here justify things (behaviors) with the culture. They always say our
> forefathers did it the same way, so why should we change? I think that if we are all
> educated things will change.

Adam, in discussing the problem of culture as an obstacle to behavior change in the community said, "People believe there is no HIV/AIDS and sometimes they think HIV/AIDS is from another town so you have to convince people of the presence of the disease in the community." On the contrary, Adam said "I believe the disease is real and that is why I am protecting myself and my family."

Also, Salifu another participant said, "My people still believe in their traditional practices of having many wives and children. They are also Muslims so on the issue of polygamy it is difficult to convince them to change their practices." On the contrary, Salifu said "Islam does not necessarily endorse polygamy. I will do all I can to protect my family because when I die of AIDS I will put the whole family into disgrace and my community will have no respect for them."

96

Abibata recalled the difficulty of her unequal power relations with the husband by stating,

"you need to understand our culture, as a second wife, I don't have much strength [power] to ask

him to stop anything. [Extra-marital affairs or use of condoms]." On the contrary it is this

unequal power relation that has provided the impetus for her to change her sexual practices.

Abibata said "I will protect myself with all the knowledge that I have but I cannot watch him 24

hours to determine what he is doing. That is just the nature of our men."

The influence of religion. The belief in Islam is strong among participants. During the

discussions, participants referred to God, the Koran, and the Bible. Nevertheless, participants

also believed in their customs and traditions so it was difficult to determine if a practice was a

religious one or was based on the culture of the area. This was what Mohammed, a participant

said on the issue of religion as an obstacle to change in sexual practices in the community:

I will say religion is a big obstacle to change. Some people believe that God brings

HIV/AIDS. HIV/AIDS is not man-made. In our community some people strongly

believe that God gives wives and not man. They cite the Prophet Mohammed as having

many wives and concubines. Some people also believe that having many children is

God's blessing.

On the contrary, Mohammed saw religion as an encouragement to practice faithfulness and

change in sexual practice because he also believed extra-marital affairs will make him

susceptible to HIV/AIDS when he explained, "I don't know the status of the woman I am

courting since she may be sleeping with another man and not telling me the truth."

Samad also said that religion was a major factor that deterred people from making changes in

their sexual practices. Samad said "one attraction of Islam is the freedom to have many wives if

you have the money and capabilities to do so, so what is the point in being a Muslim if you can't have more than one wife?"

On the other hand, Samad believes that the teachings of Islam and HIV/AIDS education simultaneously influenced his decision to adapt HIV/AIDS prevention education. Adam another participant said, "The Mallam (religious teacher) said God said we should marry and have children. So why marry and use condoms?" On the contrary Adam also said Islam also teaches that you should only marry if you have the capability to look after your wives. To Adam the knowledge that he did not have the capabilities and the education about the vectors of transmission of HIV encouraged him to make changes in his sexual practices.

Whereas, some religious beliefs deterred people from adopting desirable sexual practices to prevent HIV/AIDS, some religious beliefs also encouraged participants to make personal changes in their sexual practices. As a community, Savelugu/Nanton is predominantly a traditional society. Customs and traditions are the principal pillars upon which the society strives for survival. Participants remarked that cultural practices such as polygamy, extra-marital affairs, and the position of women deterred people from adapting desirable sexual practices to prevent HIV/AIDS. Religion and culture were identified as two factors that encouraged as well as mitigated changes in sexual practices in Savelugu/Nanton according to participants. Religion and culture can thus be described as a double-edged sword for changes in sexual practices in Savelugu/Nanton District of Ghana.

Chapter Summary

The purpose of this study was to understand how Ghanaian adults learned to make changes in their sexual practices in response to HIV/AIDS crisis. The first task was to determine changes in sexual practices. Findings indicate that all participants made changes in their sexual practices in response to the HIV/AIDS crisis. Next the researcher was interested in knowing how

98

the participants learned to make the change. The data indicate a learning process using a three phase process. [see Table 2]. In addition to learning, participants were influenced to make the change because of their cultural and religious beliefs. For example, the knowledge that his culture could not provide all the answers to HIV/AIDS prompted Salifu, a participant to make a change in his sexual practices. Secondly, the knowledge that Islam allowed polygamy was a deterrent for some people failing to make changes in their sexual practices. Finally, the fear of death and the social stigma of HIV/AIDS in the community motivated participants to seek more knowledge about HIV/AIDS that led them to the group. Once participants found this intact group, they engaged in informal learning activities about HIV/AIDS and this contributed to their change in sexual practices in response to HIV/AIDS. The sexual practices they adopted were abstinence prior to marriage, limiting the number of sexual partners, and adoption of condom use.

CHAPTER FIVE

SUMMARY, CONCLUSIONS, DISCUSSION, AND RECOMMENDATIONS

Introduction

The purpose of this study was to understand how Ghanaian adults learned to change their sexual practices in response to the HIV/AIDS crisis. To achieve this objective, the following research questions were examined.

1. What changes have Ghanaian adults made in their sexual practices since learning about HIV/AIDS?

2. How do Ghanaian adults learn formally or informally what they need to know to make changes in their sexual practices?

3. What is the learning process that leads Ghanaian adults to make changes in their sexual practices?

4. What factors encourage or deter Ghanaian adults from making changes in their sexual practices?

This chapter presents and discusses the conclusions drawn from the study. This chapter also includes discussions of the results based on the reviewed literature on HIV/AIDS behavior change models, mass media and health education, and adult learning. This chapter concludes with study implications, and recommendations for future research, and the chapter summary.

Summary of Findings

In this study I discovered five major findings. First, all the participant made changes in their sexual practices in response to HIV/AIDS. Those changes were adhering to abstinence prior

100

to marriage, limiting the number of sexual partners, and adopting condom use. The learning process that the participants experienced in making those changes includes the other four findings. First, they become initially aware of HIV/AIDS. This awareness was made possible by other people and the mass media. As a consequence of this initial awareness participants become concerned about dying from HIV/AIDS, as well as experiencing the stigma that goes along with a family member having HIV/AIDS. This fear of death and the concern over the stigma of HIV/AIDS were catalytic agents that motivated the participants to engage in further learning. The activities of the further learning included the group work and individual studies reinforced by group members. Finally, as part of the learning process discovered two factors were prominent in encouraging or deterring participants in learning about HIV/AIDS. Those two factors are the influence of culture and the influence of religion.

Conclusions and Discussions

Based on those five findings, the following conclusions were drawn from this study. First, the fear of death and societal stigma motivate engagement in learning about HIV/AIDS. Second, informal learning approaches provided initial awareness of HIV/AIDS. Third, the learning process of participants reflects the health belief and consumer information processing models of health behavior change. Fourth, further learning about HIV/AIDS was facilitated by group learning activities.

Conclusion One: Fear of death and societal stigma motivated engagement in learning about HIV/AIDS.

McCombie and Anarfi (1992) asserted that increased awareness about HIV/AIDS did not translate into adaptation of safer sex practices. This was not supported by the findings of this study. Rather data revealed that increased awareness was a catalyst for further learning and

101

hence adoption of safer sex practices. Motivation to engage in learning about HIV/AIDS was triggered by the fear of death and societal stigma about HIV/AIDS.

The catalysts identified played a significant role in helping people realize that they could bring about changes in their lives through learning to avoid the repercussions of HIV/AIDS in the community. These motivational catalysts served as a bridge of hope. People realized that though the education they received on HIV/AIDS was scary, yet it provided the missing link for people to begin to perceive a need for action. People expressed this need through group activities that taught them strategies about HIV/AIDS prevention in the community. One strategy was that they supported each other, counseled each other, and were a resource to each other. Participants also realized that HIV/AIDS was a community problem so they used community resources such as the health center resources to educate members about HIV/AIDS.

Awusabo-Asare's (1992) also asserted that traditional practices like polygamy, puberty rites, and festivals that promote sexual promiscuity also led to further spread of HIV/AIDS. This was substantiated by the findings of the study. For example, in limiting the number of sexual partners, participants were therefore aware that traditional practices such as polygamy, extra-marital affairs, and unfaithfulness in marriages were risk factors and hence vectors for acquiring the disease which had to be changed.

This conclusion supports Awusabo-Asare's (1992) assertion that traditional sexual practices were vectors for the transmission of HIV/AIDS in Ghana. By changing their sexual practices participants sought to prevent HIV/AIDS, thus recognizing that traditional sexual practices put them at risk for HIV infection.

The messages participants received from the mass media by way of posters and billboards helped reinforce the severity of HIV/AIDS in the community. The programs

102

participants heard on the radio and watched on the television all aided in creating an atmosphere showcasing the severity of the disease. In addition, numerous deaths had been reported in the community prior to my arrival in Ghana. These deaths were attributed to HIV/AIDS and further helped the community to refocus on AIDS education and prevention.

Whereas in the past the fear of death and societal stigma of HIV/AIDS were barriers to HIV/AIDS education because of lack of knowledge about HIV/AIDS transmission routes, now due to a shift in the culture as a result of new information and knowledge about HIV/AIDS, these barriers are now impetus for engaging in learning about the disease.

This conclusion reflects the findings of Hornik (2002) study. He found that behavior change will only occur when social norms change. Similar to Hornik, this researcher found a shift in the social norms in that the impact of "all die be die" was less important for participants. Whereas, historically, Ghanaians have held the belief that death is destined regardless of its form, participants in this study demonstrated a shift in teaching about the causes of death where premature death from HIV/AIDS was of concern to them.

Conclusion 2: Informal learning approaches facilitate change in sexual practices.

The study established that learning to change sexual practices by participants was predominantly informal. In discussing informal learning, McGivney (1999) sees this kind of learning as learning that takes place outside a dedicated learning environment and which arises from the activities and interests of individuals and groups but which may or may not be recognized as learning. Secondly, McGivney (1999) described informal learning as non-course based learning activities which includes discussions, talks or presentations, information, advise and guidance provided or facilitated in response to expressed interests and needs by people from a range of sectors and organizations (health, housing, social services, employment services, education and training and guidance services). Finally, McGivney (1999) described informal learning as planned and structured learning such as short courses organized in response to identified interests and needs but delivered in flexible and informal settings.

Conner (1997) defines informal learning as learning that does not occur during formal training programs. Conner(1997) argues that informal learning is a lifelong process whereby individual adults acquire attitudes, values, skills, and knowledge from daily experience and the educative influences and resources in his/her environment, from family, and neighbors, from work and play, from the market place, the library, and the mass media. The learning activities that participants engaged in and that which they described mirrored informal learning as described by McGivney (1999) and Conner (1997).

Merriam and Caffarella (1999) specifically addressed the settings of nonformal learning as settings that include community-based learning opportunities or indigenous learning. This was precisely the kind of environment in which group members engaged whilst learning to make changes in their sexual practices.

Merriam and Caffarella (1999) also describe informal learning contexts as situations where learning occurs in the learner's natural setting and is initiated by the learner. Based on these insights, this study supports the conclusion that most learning by participants was informal learning.

The findings about informal learning support the cultural belief of the people. For example, there is the belief that what is private should not be discussed in the open. Sex generally is never discussed in the open in Africa.

In Ghana until now it was difficult to discuss sex in the open. HIV/AIDS has changed that and has forced communities to come together to understand the nature of the disease.

104

However, this openness is not yet widespread to allow communities to have open dialogues on HIV/AIDS. This represents another observable cultural shift. Informal settings, such as market squares, homes, and places where privacy and confidentiality are assured to some extent provide good spaces for people. This probably explains why informal approaches to learning were important for this group. In addition, the adult learning literature provides good examples of informal learning settings for adults, such as travel, grocery stores, book clubs, churches, and mosques.

The personal nature of HIV/AIDS also suggests that people will always have the need for some form of confidentiality to dialogue about the disease. Informal settings for the group provided the comfort of space where members were able to talk freely about the disease and also learn about the disease.

Conclusion 3: The process of learning about HIV/AIDS that leads to change in sexual practices reflects the health belief model and the consumer information processing model.

McCormack, (1999) believes that learning to change a health behavior is the result of perceived susceptibility and severity of threat of disease condition. According to the health belief model, a person's motivation to undertake a health behavior is a combination of individual perception about the disease, modifying behaviors, and the likelihood of action.

The findings suggest that these individuals clearly perceived susceptibility and severity of threat of disease. For example, they were worried about the societal stigma of the disease and were afraid of death. They therefore found means of mitigating the severity by engaging in learning activities that promoted good sexual practices. These good sexual practices were the use of protection prior to engaging in sexual activities, and limiting the number of sexual partners as well as using condoms.

There are two assumptions of the consumer information processing model that are important for our discussion in relation to the findings of the study. First, individuals are limited to how much information they can process and second, in order to increase the usability of information, individuals must combine little pieces of information into chunks for faster recall and use. Applied to HIV/AIDS education, CIP stipulates that the information must be available, be useful, and be in a friendly format. In addition, the most effective medium for communication must be chosen for the message.

The assumption is that an effective delivery medium will aid in information usage and recall. The model also assumes that information should be designed for a particular target audience and placed conveniently for their use. This has implications for non-western and non-literate societies. As already mentioned Ghana has over 42 local languages and only 5 are used for national broadcast on radio and television. The non-usage of a language on national television has implication for programs that use mass media channels for dissemination.

According to Bettman and McGuire (1979) information environment affects how easily people obtain, process, and use information. Thus this model stipulates that the location, format, readability and ability to process relevant information are essential for the adoption of healthy behavior. Since Ghana boasts many ethnic groups and languages, the challenge of this model will be the extent to which messages catered to people living with AIDS. This model underscores the importance of information and relevancy to match the level of comprehension and relevancy.

The process of learning appear to reflect basic adult learning principles of self directed learning, goal oriented learning, adults are practical, adults enter in to a learning process with a task centered orientation to learning, adults are motivated to learn by intrinsic and extrinsic motivation, and that adults come to a learning situation with a wealth of experience and

106

knowledge. Finally, participants were empowered to engage the community in this all important social educative process about HIV/AIDS because of their learning accomplishments.

Conclusion 4: Group support encourages change in sexual practices

First, all members of the group were involved in the planning process of what they wanted to dialogue about in their group discussions. This is a cardinal principle of adult learning that was adhered to, and may have helped in the team building spirit that the participants amply demonstrated.

Second, there was a culture of mutual respect among members of the group. Members respected the privacy of each other especially about their HIV status. This fostered open communication among members leading to effective learning.

The author observed a spirit of collaboration in the learning process, in that any member could lead group discussions and was free to bring any topic of interest to the table for group discussion. In this way individuals saw learning as a group process and not the sole prerogative of one person. It also drew on the previous experiences of members and demonstrated how mutually beneficial learning was to all. By not only drawing on the past experiences of members, but the diversity of the group in age, status, educational attainment, occupation, and other life experiences, members were able to dialogue on issues affecting the community from different perspectives. This promoted critical reflective thinking and further enhanced the learning activities of the group.

There was shared learning by members of the group. Men and women came together under one umbrella to discuss sex and sexual practices in the open. This was a cultural shift in the community. Men and women became equal partners in learning about HIV/AIDS help break down cultural beliefs about gender ascribed roles for women and men. There was a sense that

HIV/AIDS was community malice and not just one individual or family, hence community effort was needed to eradicate HIV/AIDS.

Implications

People are generally motivated because of need to satisfy a demand or purpose. For example, adults undertake a project to address a need or solve a problem. Many adult students go back to school as a result of the need for promotion or personal satisfaction. In most cases the information available to adults is not traumatic or based on scare tactics. In this case practitioners' use of health educational materials that warned of the fatal consequences from unprotected sexual activities did at least get the attention of people and provided an opportunity to help people learn and come to realize that there is hope in the midst of the devastation of HIV/AIDS. The value of this strategy was to get the attention of the community. This attention was desirable in leading to learning about HIV/AIDS and subsequently changes in sexual practices.

Overwhelmingly participants reported that the fear of death and societal stigma of HIV/AIDS actually motivated them to learn about HIV/AIDS. This finding suggests that adult educators and health educators can tailor their educational messages about diseases to emphasize unpalatable consequences in the hope of drawing attention to important health problems such as HIV/AIDS. Once people perceive the health problem as severe, they will begin to learn and ask for information that will help them address the health issue in the hope of complete eradication. This strategy could be adopted in settings dealing with chronic but preventable ailments such as malaria, obesity, and other diseases that adult health educators are confronted with daily.

Educators need to be aware that cultural beliefs and their influence on people's behavior in Africa are waning. There is widespread perception among Africans that there is a cultural shift

108

in beliefs and attitudes with regards to diseases. This may be due to increased awareness and knowledge about diseases. For example, in the past "all die be die" was predominant but today "all die be die" is no more acceptable as an explanation for the numerous deaths that occur daily as a result of HIV/AIDS. This cultural shift has implications for AIDS educators.

Adult educators need to assist stakeholders' value indigenous knowledge of communities affected by HIV/AIDS. Adult educators must also help stakeholders place the interests of communities dealing with HIV/AIDS at the center of their instructional deliveries. This will help communities identify more with HIV/AIDS educational materials in the hope that it will produce the desired changes in sexual practices.

Second, adult educators need to assist communities fighting HIV/AIDS, by utilizing informal adult learning activities. This study demonstrated the importance of informal education such as discussions in groups, the market square, and other public places, as well as inviting experts to make informal presentations on pertinent issues.

Third, the process of learning suggests targeted instruction as well as spacing of instruction to account for the levels of understanding and level of reading. This will further assist people in learning to make changes in their sexual practices to prevent HIV/AIDS.

Recommendations for Future Research

Four recommendations for future research are evident from this study. First, this study examined learning of an intact group. There are other social groups that are not intact groups. There is the need to examine if people are learning outside of an intact group and how they are learning. This will help educators determine or compare what factors promote learning in an intact group versus learning of individuals outside of interest groups.

109

Second, this study examined learning in a setting in close proximity to an urban area,

there is the need to examine if there is a difference in how people learn about HIV/AIDS in a

rural area as compared to an urban area. This is because in Africa the farther away a community

is from an urban center the harder it is to get information about health and education. The mass

media is Africa is not geographically adequately distributed. There are more radio stations,

television stations, newspapers, magazines, and billboards in the urban centers than in the rural

areas. Access to information is difficult in the rural areas as compared to the urban areas, thus a

study that addresses these dichotomies would add to our understanding of adult learning in social

contexts.

Third, this study uncovered learning approaches in an informal settings as appropriate for

learning to change sexual practices. There may be other learning approaches that may be

germane to changes in sexual practices that need to be examined. For example, how learning

associated with formal settings help situate HIV/AIDS discourse in Africa in view of the cultural

challenges would add to our understanding of adult learning.

Fourth this study uncovered two catalysts for motivating people to learn about

HIV/AIDS. There might be other catalysts that focus on other motivating factors that this study

did not identify. A future study that addresses these catalysts will add to our understanding of

learning in adulthood.

REFERENCES

Adih, W., & Alexander, C. (1999). Determinants of condom use to prevent HIV

infection among youth in Ghana. Journal of Adolescent Health, 24, 63-72.

Ajzen, I. (1991). The theory of planned behavior. Organizational behavior and human

Decision Processes, 50, 179-211.

Ajzen, I., & Fishbein, M. (1980). Understanding the attitudes and predicting social

behavior. Englewood Cliffs, NJ: Prentice-Hall.

Anarfi, J. K. (1993). Sexuality, migration and AIDS in Ghana - A socio-behavioral

study. In J. C. Caldwell, G. Santow, I. O. Orubuloye, P. Caldwell & J. K. Anarfi. (Eds.),

Sexual networking and HIV/AIDS in West Africa. Supplement to Health Transition

Review 3. (pp. 45-68). Canberra: Australian National University.

Anarfi, J. K. (2000). Universities and HIV/AIDS in Sub-Saharan Africa: A case study of

the University of Ghana, Legon. New York: The World Bank.

Anarfi, J. K., & Antwi, P. (1993). Sexual networking in a high-risk environment of

street-involved youth in Accra city and its implications for the spread of HIV/AIDS.

Paper presented at Workshop on Social Dimensions of AIDS in Africa, University of

Cape Coast, Ghana, 18-20 October.

Anarfi, J. K., & Antwi, P. (1995). Street youth in Accra city. Sexual networking in high risk-

environment and its implications for the spread of HIV/AIDS. In I. O. Orubuloye (Ed.),

The third World AIDS Epidemic. Health Transition Review 5 (supplement), Canberra:

Australian National University.

111

Anarfi, J. K., & Awusabo-Asare, K. (1993). Experimental research on sexual networking

in some selected areas of Ghana. In J. C. Caldwell, G. Santow, I. O. Orubuloye, P.

Caldwell and J. K. Anarfi (Eds.), Sexual networking and HIV/AIDS in West Africa.

Supplement to Health Transition Review 3 (pp. 29-44). Canberra: Australian National

University.

Anarfi, J. K., Appiah, E. N., & Awusabo-Asare, K. (1997). Livelihood and the risk of

HIV/AIDS infection in Ghana. The case of female itinerant traders. In J.C. Caldwell, Gigi

Santow, I. O. Orubuloye, P. Caldwell, & J. K. Anarfi (Eds.), Sexual networking and HIV

in West Africa (pp. 225-242). Canberra: Australian National University.

Archie-Booker, E. (1996). The politics of planning culturally relevant AIDS education

for African-American women. Unpublished doctoral dissertation, University of Georgia.

Athens.

Aspinwall, L. G., Kemeny, M. E., Taylor, S. E., Schneider, S. G., & Dudley, J. P.

(1991). Predictors of gay men's AIDS risk-reduction behavior. Health Psychology, 10,

432-444.

Atkin, C. K., & Rice, R. E. (Eds.). (2001). Public communication campaigns. (3rd ed.).

Thousand Oaks, CA: Sage.

Awusabo-Asare, K. (1995). HIV/AIDS education and counseling experiences from

Ghana. Health Transition Review 5, (Supplement), 229-236.

Awusabo-Asare, K., & Anarfi, J. K. (1997). Health seeking behavior of persons with

HIV/AIDS in Ghana. Health Transition Review 7, (Supplement.), 243-256.

Awusabo-Asare, K. & Anarfi, J. K. (1999a). Routes to HIV transmission and

intervention: An analytic framework. The Continuing African HIV/AIDS Epidemic, pp 1-

112

9. Health Transition Center: Canberra. The Australian National University.

Awusabo-Asare, K., & Anarfi, J. K. (1999b). Rethinking the circumstances surrounding the

first sexual experience in the era of AIDS in Ghana. The continuing African HIV/AIDS

epidemic. Health Transition Center: Canberra. Australia.

Backer, T. E., Rogers, E. M., Sopory, P. (1992). Designing health communication

campaigns: What works? Newbury Park: Sage.

Baffour-Ankomah. (1999). AIDS, the deadly deception exposed. [Review of the book

AIDS, the failure of contemporary science] Fourth Estate, London UK

Bandura, A. (1977).Social learning theory. Englewood Cliffs, NJ: Prentice-Hall.

Bandura, A. (1986). Social foundations of thought and action: A social cognitive theory.

Englewood Cliffs, NJ: Prentice-Hall.

Bandura, A. (1989). Social cognitive theory. In R. Vasta (Ed), Annals of Child Development. 6,

1-60. Greenwich, CT: Jai Press Ltd.

Baumgartner, L. M. (2000). The incorporation of HIV/AIDS into identity over time.

Unpublished doctoral dissertation, The University of Georgia, Athens.

Baumgartner, L. M., Courtenay, B. C., Merriam, S. B., & Reeves, P. M. (2000). HIV-positive

adults perspective transformation over time. Conference on Qualitative Research in

Education. Athens, Georgia, January 2000.

Bettman, J. R. (1979). An information processing theory of consumer choice. Reading,

MA: Addison-Wesley.

Bettman, J. R., & McGuire, W, J. (1979). Public communication as a strategy for

inducing health promotion behavioral change. Preventive Medicine, 13, 299-319.

Bogdan, R. C., & Biklen, S. K. (1998). Qualitative research for education: An introduction to theory and methods. Boston, MA: Allyn and Bacon

Bogdan, R. C., & Biklen, S. K. (1992). Qualitative research for education. Boston,

MA: Allyn and Bacon.

Bollinger, L., & Antwi, P. (1999). The economic impact of AIDS in Ghana. New York:

The Futures Group

Bosompra, K. (1998). Psychosocial determinants of condom use among Ghanaian

students: Application of the theory of planned behavior and health belief model.

Unpublished doctoral Dissertation, The University of Massachusetts, Amherst.

Bosompra, K. (1989). Dissemination of health information among rural dwellers of

Africa: A Ghanaian experience. Social Science and Medicine, 29, 1133-1140.

Brown, W., DiClemente, R. J., & Reynolds, M. A. (1992). Culture and HIV

Education: Reaching high risk heterosexuals in Asian-American communities. Journal of

Applied Communication Research, 20, 275-292.

Burgess, R. G. (Ed.). (1982). Field research: A source book and field manual. London:

G. Allen & Unwin.

Caldwell, J. C. (2000). Rethinking the African AIDS epidemic. Population and

Development Review, 26, 185-234.

Campbell, A. L. (2001). Human immunodeficiency virus prevention education: An

Evaluation of the impact of AIDS "101" on HIV-related knowledge and attitudes towards

people with HIV. Unpublished doctoral dissertation, The University of Georgia, Athens.

Centers for Disease Control and Prevention. (1981). Morbidity and Mortality Weekly Report.

MMWR, 30(21): 1-3.

Centers for Disease Control and Prevention. (1995). HIV/AIDS Surveillance Report, 6-1-120

Atlanta, Georgia: US Department of Health and Human Services.

Centers for Disease Control and Prevention. (1999). HIV/AIDS Surveillance Report, 6-

1-139. Atlanta Georgia: U.S. Department of Health and Human Services.

Centers for Disease Control and Prevention. (2000). Stabilization of AIDS in the US.

Milestones in the U.S. HIV epidemic. Retrieved July2, 2005

http://www.cdcnpin.org/scripts/News/NewsList.asp?strTempOrLive=Live

Centers for Disease Control and Prevention. (2002). HIV/AIDS Surveillance Report.

Midyear edition. 12(1). American Public Health.

Centers for Disease Control and Prevention. (2005). Fact Sheet on HIV/AIDS prevention (2005).

Retrieved May 20, 2005

http://www.cdc.gov/omh/AMH/factsheets/hiv.htm

Conner, M. L. (1997). Informal learning. Retrieved May 5, 2005, from

http://www.agelesslearner.com/intros/informal.html

Congressional Research Service Report (CRS) (2002). AIDS in Africa. Retrieved June

26, 2002 from http://cnie.org/NLE/CRSreports/international/inter-34.cfm

Courtenay, B. C., Merriam, S. B., & Reeves, P. M. (1999). The centrality of meaning

–making in transformational learning. How HIV-positive adults make sense of their

lives. Adult Education Quarterly, 48 (2), 65-84.

Decosas, J., & Adrien, A. (1999). Migration and HIV. AIDS, 77-84.

Dench, S., & Regan, J. (1999). Learning in later life: motivation and impact. DFEE

Research Report RR 183. Institute for Employment Studies. UK.

Denzin, N. K. (1970). The research act, a theoretical introduction to sociological

Methods. Chicago: Aldine Pub. Company.

115

DiClemente, R. J. (1996). Psychosocial determinants of condom use among

    Adolescents: In R. J. DiClemente (Ed.), Adolescents and AIDS: A generation in jeopardy

    (pp. 34-51). Newbury Park, CA: Sage.

DiClemente, R. J. (1993). Epidemiology of AIDS, HIV seroprevalence and HIV

    incidence among adolescents. Journal of School Health, 10, 204-210.

Douglas, B., & Moustakas, C. (1985). Heuristic inquiry: the internal search to know. Journal of

    Humanistic Psychology, 25, 33-55.

Elder, J. P. (2001). Behavior change and public health in the developing world.

    Thousand Oaks, CA: Sage.

Emma, Ross. (2002, November 27). HIV hits as many women as men. The Atlanta

    Journal and Constitution, pp. A1, A14.

Feldman, G. (Ed.). (1990). Culture and AIDS. New York: Praeger.

Fishbien, M. (1982). Behavioral science and public health: A necessary partnership for

    Prevention. Public Health Reports, 111 (Supplement 1), 5-10.

Fisher, W. A. (1984). Predicting contraceptive behavior among university men:

    Theories of emotions and behavioral intentions. Journal of Applied Social Psychology,

    14, 104-123.

Freire, P. (1972). Pedagogy of the oppressed. New York: Continuum.

Ghana AIDS cases continue to increase.(2003). HIV/AIDS Update. Ghana AIDS

    Commission Newsletter 1(1), 15-20. Accra: Ghana.

Ghana News Agency. (4 April, 2001). About 600 people infected with AIDS in Ghana.

    Retrieved August 17, 2001 from http://www.Ghanaweb.com

Ghana Press (April 25, 2005). AIDS cases continue to climb. Retrieved May 10, 2005 from http://www.ghanaweb.com

Glesne, C. (1999). Becoming qualitative researchers: an introduction. (2nd ed.). New

York: Longman.

Glasser, B. G., & Srauss, A. L. (1967). Discovery of grounded theory: Strategies for

qualitative research. Chicago: AVC.

Graeff, J., Elder, J., & Mills Booth, E. (1993). Communication for health and behavior

change. A developing country perspective. San Francisco: Jossey-Bass.

Gottfried, R. (1983). The black death. Natural and human disaster in medieval

Europe. New York: Free Press.

Hill, R. J. (2004). AIDS, empire, and the US politics of giving. Convergence, 37(4), 59-

72.

Hochbaum, G. M. (1958). Health behavior. Belmont, CA: Wadsworth Publication

Company.

Hope, K. R. Sr., (Eds.). (1999). AIDS and development in Africa: A social science

Perspective. NY: Haworth Press.

Hornik, R. C. (2002). Public health communication: Evidence for behavior change.

Mahwah NJ: Lawrence Erlbaum Associates

Houle, C. O. (1964). Continuing your education. New York: McGraw-Hill

Janz, N. K., & Becker, M. K. (1984). The health belief model: A decade later. Health

Education Quarterly, 11, 1-47.

Kelly, J. (1994). Sexually transmitted disease prevention: approaches that work.

interventions to reduce risk behavior among individuals, groups, and

Communities. Sex Transm Disease 21(2 supplement). S73-75.

Kelly, J. (1995a). Advances in HIV/AIDS education and prevention. Family Relations

44, 345-352.

Kelly, J. (1995b). Changing HIV Risk Behavior: Practical Strategies. New York:

Guilford.

Knowles, M. S. (1980). The modern practice of adult education: From pedagogy to

andragogy. New York: Cambridge.The Adult Education Company.

Konotey-Ahulu, F. (1989). What is AIDS? Worcester: Tetteh-A' Domeno Pub.

Krathwohl, D. R.(1998). Methods of educational and social science research: An

Integrated approach (2nd ed.). New York: Longman.

Lindeman, E. C. (1926). The meaning of adult education. New York: New Republic,

Inc.

Mann, J., Tarantola, D., & Netter, T. (1996). AIDS in the world: A global report.

Cambridge, MA: Harvard University Press.

Matheson, S. (1988). Why triangulate? Educational Researcher, 17(2), 13-17

McCormack, A. S. (1999). Revisiting college student knowledge and attitudes about

HIV/AIDS, 1987, 1991, and 1995. College Student Journal, 31(3), 356-363

McCombie, S., Anarfi, J. K.(1992). Evaluation of mass media campaign to prevent

AIDS among young people in Ghana. 1991-1992. AIDS Technical Support.

Public health communication contract #DPE5972-200-7070-00 Washington DC.

United States Agency for International Development (USAID).

McCombie, S., Hornik, R.; Anarfi, J. (2002). Effects of a mass media campaign to prevent

AIDS among young people in Ghana. In R. C. Hornik (ed). Public health

communication: Evidence for behavior change. Mahwah, NJ: Lawrence Erlbaum.

118

McGivney, M. L. (1999). Informal learning in the community: A trigger for change and

   development. Leicester: NIACE. 99+ xii pages. Report of the DFEE funded study that

   focuses on the role of informal learning in starting people learning pathways. Retrieved

   May 5, 2005 from

   http://www.infed.org/biblio/inf-lrn.htm.

McGuire, T. (1981). Theoretical Foundations of public communication campaigns. IN

   R. Rice and W. Paisky (Eds.). Public communication campaign. Beverly Hill CA: Sage.

Merriam, S. B., & Simpson, E. L. (1995). A guide to research for Educators and Trainers of

   Adults. (2nd ed.), Malabar, FL: Krieger.

Merriam, S. B. (1998). Qualitative research and case study applications in education

   (2nd ed.), San Francisco: Jossey-Bass.

Merriam, S. B. and Cafferella, R. S. (1999). Learning in adulthood: A comprehensive

   Guide. San Francisco: Jossey-Bass.

Mill, J. & Anarfi, J K. (2002). HIV Risk Environment for Ghanaian women:

   Challenges to prevention. Social Science & Medicine, 54,325-337.

Morgan, D. L. (1988) Focus groups as qualitative research (2nd Ed.). Newbury Park,

   CA: Sage.

Moustakas, C. E. (1990). Heuristic research: design, methodology and applications.

   Newbury Park: Sage Publication.

Neequaye, J. E. (1988). Ghanaian children and women infected with

   Immunodeficiency virus (HIV). Ghana Medical Journal, 22 (3): 86-89

Neequaye, A. R., Neequaye, J. E. & Biggar, R. J. (1991). Factors that could influence the

   spread of AIDS in Ghana, West Africa. AIDS, 4, 914-919.

Oruboloye, I., (1993). African families and AIDS: context, reactions and potential

Interventions. Health Transition Review 3, 1-14

Oruboloye, I., Caldwell, C., & Caldwell, P. (1993). African women's control over their

sexuality in an era of AIDS: a study of the Yoruba of Nigeria. Health Transition Review

3, 14-28.

Panford, S., Nyaney, M., Amoah Opoku, S., & Garbrah Aidoo, N. (2001). Using folk

Media in HIV/AIDS prevention in rural Ghana. American Journal of Public Health: 91.

1559-1562.

Panos Institute. (1999). AIDS hits African women hardest. Retrieved September 17, 2001 from

the World Wide Web at http://www.oneworld.org/panos/news/aidsspec2.html.

Patton, M. Q. (1990). Qualitative evaluation and research in methods (2d Ed).

Newbury Park, CA: Sage.

Patton, M. Q. (2002). Qualitative research and evaluation methods (3rd Ed.). Thousand

Oaks, CA: Sage.

Petosa, R. & Jackson, K. (1991). Using the health belief model to predict safer sex

intentions among adolescent. Health Education Quarterly, 18, 463-476.

Prochaska, J. O, & DiClemente, C. C. (1983). Stages and processes of self-change of

Smoking: towards an integrative model of change. Journal of Consulting Clinical

Psychology: 1, 390-395.

Rosenstock, I., Strecher, V., & Becker, M. (1994).The Health Belief Model and HIV

Risk behavior change. In R. J. DiClemente, and J. L. Peterson (Eds.), Preventing

AIDS: Theories and Methods of Behavioral Interventions (pp.5-24). New York: Plenum

Press.

Rwegera, D. (1999). The African epicenter: a slow match forward. The UNESCO

Courier, October, pp. 22-24.

Sessions, K. (1998). Living outside the circle. The politics of HIV/AIDS education and

The disenfranchisement of HIV-negative Gay men. Unpublished doctoral dissertation.

The University of Georgia. Athens.

Siegal, H. A. (1990). Intravenous drug abuse and the HIV epidemic in two Midwestern

Cities. A preliminary report. Journal of Drug Issues. 20 (2): 281-290.

Stake, R. E. (1995).The art of case study research: perspectives on practice. Thousand

Oaks, CA: Sage Publication.

Thorndike, E. L., Bregman, E. O., Tilton Warren, J., & Woodyard, E. (1928). Adult

Learning. New York: The McMillan Company.

Tough, A, L. (1971) Adult learning. New York: The Macmillan Company.

Topouzis, D. (1998).The implications of HIV/AIDS for rural development policy and

program focus on Sub-Saharan Africa, Study Paper. No. 6 United Nations Development

Program.

Ugugi, E. N., Simonseon, J. N., & Bosine, M. (1999). Prevention of transmission of

HIV in Africa: effectiveness of condom promotion and health education among

Prostitutes. Lancet: 870-887.

Umeh, D. (Ed.). (1999). Confronting the AIDS epidemic: Cross cultural perspectives on

HIV/AIDS Education. Trenton, NJ. Africa World Press.

UNAIDS (2005a). Epidemiological fact sheet on HIV/AIDS and sexually transmitted

infections by country. Available: http://www.unaids.org

UNAIDS (2005b). Report on the global HIV/AIDS epidemic. Geneva, Switzerland:

Joint United Nations Programme on HIV/AIDS.

UNAIDS (2002) epidemiological fact sheet on HIV/AIDS and sexually

Transmitted diseases. Geneva, Switzerland: UNAIDS Joint United Nations Program on

HIV/AIDS.

UNAIDS (2001). Report on the global HIV/AIDS epidemic: June 2001. Geneva,

Switzerland: UNAIDS Joint United Nations Programme on HIV/AIDS and WHO

UNAIDS (2000). Report on the global HIV/AIDS epidemic. Geneva, Switzerland:

UNAIDS Joint United Nations Programme on HIV/AIDS.

UNAIDS. (1999). The response to AIDS in Ghana. Joint United Nations Development

Program on HIV/AIDS. Accra, Ghana.

UNICEF- Progress of Nations Report (2000). My song against AIDS. Retrieved June 10,

2002 from http://www.unicef.org/pon00/datas.htm

UNAIDS (1998). Ghana: epidemiological fact sheet on HIV/AIDS and sexually

Transmitted diseases. Geneva, Switzerland: UNAIDS Joint United Nations Program on

HIV/AIDS.

United Nations Development Program. (1997). Human development report, New York: Oxford

University Press.

United Nations Development Program. (1999). Human development report, New York: Oxford

University Press.

United Nations Development Program. (2000). Human development report, New York: Oxford

University Press.

Wingwood, G., & DiClemente, R. (1992). Cultural, gender, and psychological

Influences on HIV-related behavior of African American female adolescents:

122

Implications for the development of tailored prevention programs. Ethnicity and

Disease, 2, 381-388.

AIDS in Africa: Washington Post (December 12, 1999).

Wolf, R., & Bond, K. (2002). Exploring similarity between peer educators and their

Contacts and AIDS-protective behaviors in reproductive health programs for

Adolescents and young adults in Ghana. AIDS Care, 14: 3, 361-373.

World AIDS Conference (2002). Available at

http://www.hdnet.org/library/barcelona_newspapers/thursday_english.pdf

World Bank (1999a). Confronting AIDS: Public Priorities in a Global Epidemic,

Summary, Washington D. C.: The World Bank.

World Bank (1999b). Entering the 21st century. World Development Report-1999

New York: Oxford University Press.

Zhu, T.F., Korber, B. T.; Nahmias, A. J.; Hopper, E. P.; Sharp, P. M.; & Ho, D. D. (1998).

An African HIV-Sequence from 1959 and implications for the origin of the epidemic.

Nature, 39, 594-597.

APPENDICES

I, _____xxxx_____, agree to participate in a research study titled "the importance of learning for changing sexual practices in response to HIV/AIDS crisis in Ghana" conducted by Augustine M. Amenyah from the Department of Adult Education at the University of Georgia (542-2214) under the direction of Dr. Bradley C. Courtenay, Department of Adult Education, University of Georgia (542-4012). I understand that my participation is voluntary. I can stop taking part without giving any reason, and without penalty. I can ask to have all of the information about me returned to me, removed from the research records, or destroyed.

The reason for this study is to understand how Ghanaian adults learn to make changes in their sexual practices in response to HIV/AIDS crisis in Ghana.

If I volunteer to take part in this study, I will be asked to do the following things:
1) Answer questions about how I become aware of HIV/AIDS, what I did once I became aware, what I did to make changes in my sexual practices, how I have sustained the changes I made and what factors encouraged or deterred me from making changes in my sexual practices.
2) My information will be kept confidential and will not be disclosed to anyone without my consent and approval.

I will not receive any compensation for participating in this study.

No risk is expected as a result of my participation in this study. No information about me, or provided by me during the research, will be shared with others without my written permission, except if it is necessary to protect my welfare (for example, if I were injured and need physician care) or if required by law. I will be assigned a pseudonym for the purposes of confidentiality.

The investigator will answer any further questions about the research, now or during the course of the project (542-2214).

I understand that I am agreeing by my signature on this form to take part in this research project and understand that I will receive a signed copy of this consent form for my records.

Augustine M Amenyah_____   _____xxx_____
_____xx_____
    Name of Researcher   Signature   Date

Telephone: _706-613-3986_____
Email: _aug@uga.edu_____

__xxx_____   __xx_____
  xx_____
Name of Participant   Signature   Date

Please sign both copies, keep one and return one to the researcher.

Additional questions or problems regarding your rights as a research participant should be addressed to The Chairperson, Institutional Review Board, University of Georgia, 612 Boyd Graduate Studies Research Center, Athens, Georgia 30602-7411; Telephone (706) 542-3199; E-Mail Address IRB@uga.edu

APPENDIX B: INTERVIEW QUESTIONS

1. When did you learn about HIV/AIDS?

2. How did you learn about HIV/AIDS?

3. Explain how you first learned about HIV/AIDS?

4. How long was it after you learned about HIV/AIDS before you made a change in your sexual practices?

5. Would you explain how what you learned about HIV/AIDS influenced the change you made in your sexual practice?

6. What other factors influenced the change you made in your sexual practices?

7. Describe the change?

8. When did you decide to make the change in your sexual practices?

9. How did you make these changes in your sexual practices?

10. Enumerate some of these sexual practices?

11. What other specific sexual practices have you adopted because of the need to prevent HIV/AIDS?

12. Of all the ways you have learned about HIV/AIDS, which one(s) influenced the changes in your sexual practices?

13. What other factors influenced the change you made in your sexual practices?

14. What did you do to consolidate the changes in your sexual practices?

Printed by Books on Demand GmbH, Norderstedt / Germany